All about the
English Springer Spaniel

Frontispiece   Larkstoke Avocet. Winner at championship shows, working tests and Best Performance of the Day at the Show Spaniel Field Day.

All about the
English Springer Spaniel

OLGA M. C. HAMPTON

PELHAM BOOKS

First published in Great Britain by
Pelham Books Ltd
44 Bedford Square
London W.C.1
1980

Hampton, Olga M.C.
  All about the English springer Spaniel
    1. English springer spaniels
    I. Title
    636.7'52   SF429.E7
    ISBN 0 7207 1274 2

Typeset by Granada Graphics Ltd and printed and
bound in Singapore

To
my husband, Ian

Contents

List of Illustrations

Photographs

Frontispiece Larkstoke Avocet

Line Drawings

Line drawings by Denis Manton

Photo credits

Anne Roslin-Williams: frontispiece, 6, 7, 9, 10, 21, 22, 26, 27; Thomas Fall: 5; F. W. Simms: 13; C. M. Cooke: 16, 23; Ken Grant: 19; B. J. Harris Photography: 20; Wilson Stephens: 24, 25; Claire Lauriot: 28; Ronald Sandiford: 1.

Acknowledgements

The author is grateful to the Kennel Club for permission to reproduce the Breed Standard on Page 17*et seq* and to Mr Wilson Stephens for permission to quote from his article in *The Field* which appears on page 65. The author is also grateful to the English Springer Spaniel Club for permission to reproduce the drawing on page 18 and to the Spaniel Club Français for permission to adopt certain line drawings used in the text relating to conformation and movement.

1 History of the Breed

Archaeologists have provided us with indications that dog was companion to man way back in time, certainly as long ago as the beginning of recorded history. The stone carvings of the Ancient Egyptians portray Pharaoh with his hunting hounds and these dogs are ancestors of the present day Pharaoh Hounds. All these early recordings indicate that man used his dogs to run down the game and none of them looked of Spaniel type.

Our early ancestors hunted with the hawk and it is possible that our Roman conquerors imported a different type of dog which would work in co-operation with the hawks by flushing the game from bushes and marshland. At this time, Spain was also occupied by the Roman Legions and it could be that this new type of dog came from that region and took its name from the Latin for Spain which is *Hispania* or even from the French *Espagnol*. There are recordings of dogs specifically called Spaniels by AD 450 and the work of Spaniels is recorded in a number of documents prepared in the time of the Plantagenets. Around this time the Spaniel appears to have been much used in France but it is not until the end of the sixteenth century that the word 'Springer' is used in English Literature to indicate the particular type of dog used to flush game for the hawk and hound and net. The description 'Springer Spaniel' gradually became more widely used but it did not refer to any variety but rather to all those dogs that 'sprang' their game and all the land Spaniels could be so described.

As man's working life had been influenced by discovery and his inventive ingenuity, so has his recreation. The discovery of gunpowder and the development of the gun for sporting purposes brought a new importance to the 'springing' Spaniels. They could now be used to work in front of the hunter to flush game for the gun. Perhaps the danger signal for our breed began to flash at this stage as a degree of specialisation became apparent. Before long the sportsman was looking for a dog to act as a retriever for the game he had shot and we should be quite definite that our 'Springer Spaniel' is a dual purpose dog in the field.

At the beginning of the nineteenth century a special strain of Spaniel was developed by the Boughey family in Shropshire. The strain was

A Spaniel of 1828 from a painting by Reinagle.

carefully bred and the family maintained a Stud Book known as the *Aqualate Stud Book* to record their breeding programme. After a century of selective breeding a Springer was born in 1903 that was to become famous as Field Trial Champion Velox Powder.

Towards the end of the nineteenth century great interest centred on the working abilities of Spaniels and this was encouraged by the patronage of the nobility and county gentlemen. The Sandringham kennels of King Edward VII contained many Springers and for some considerable time these were known as Norfolk Spaniels. Some years ago when we lived in Ebrington in Gloucestershire the Earl Fortescue, who lived in the local manor, used to exercise his dogs near our house and often stopped to chat. His strain of Springers was descended from a Spaniel given to him by King Edward VII from the Sandringham Kennels.

A Sporting Spaniel Club had now been established and in 1899 the first Field Trial was held in Derbyshire. Unfortunately, Springers did not figure in the awards. At the end of the same year, a second Trial was held and again Springers were not placed in the major awards. It is interesting to contrast this with the present day when English Springers dominate the A. V. Spaniel Stakes at all the Trials.

The Spaniel Club was founded in 1885 but was second in the field as far as the organisation of Field Trials was concerned. The first Trial organised by this Club was not held until 1900 and first place was awarded to a Clumber Spaniel. The following year, the Spaniel Club organised its second Field Trial and on that occasion a Springer called Tring was placed first in the Open Stake but it was not until 1913 that an English Springer gained its title as Field Trial Champion. This dog was Rivington Sam, bred and owned by Mr C. A. Phillips.

In 1902 the Kennel Club recognised the English Springer as a specific variety of Spaniel and accorded the breed separate classification. Soon the breed had bench champions; the first dog was Mr Winton Smith's Beechgrove Will and the first bitch was Major Harry Jones' Fansom. These bench champions were much nearer the original Springer type than many of the Show Champions of today. Unfortunately both the show and working enthusiasts have adopted breeding plans that have exaggerated certain characteristics and in so doing have almost divided the English Springer into two separate types. All the early pioneers of the breed held strongly to the view that the Springer is essentially a working dog. To emphasise this point I would use an ancient misquote 'looks without work avail nothing' and a more modern quote from a current Field Trial Judge ''andsome is as 'andsome does'.

Holders of such views owned some famous prefixes and amongst them were Avendale (Duke of Hamilton), Rivington (Mr C. A. Phillips), Denne (Mr C. C. Eversfield), Beechgrove (Mr Winton Smith), Laverstoke (Lady Portal), Horsford (Mr Wm. Humphrey), L'ile (Mr D. MacDonald), Banchory (Lady Howe), Chrishall (Mr J. Kent), Glennewton (Mr J. Forbes), Matford (Mr E. E. Trimble), O'Vara (Mr Selwyn C. Jones), Inveresk (Mr McNab Chassels).

The English Springer Spaniel Club was founded in 1921 and Mr William Humphreys became its first Secretary. It is the oldest and senior Club for the breed and has always been concerned that the working qualities should be fostered and maintained at the highest possible level. Since it was founded the Club has had nine Secretaries. Of these, the first seven were enthusiasts for the working side; the eighth showed an interest in both bench and field events. The ninth Secretary was myself and I was in office for some twenty-five years, almost half the life of the Club itself. It has always been my ambition to narrow the divergence in type between the show and working dog. I am firmly of the opinion that both could be brought back nearer the type bred by the pioneers in the breed. As a judge I handle so many dogs in the ring today that show very little intelligence in expression and seem completely indifferent to their surroundings. I like a dog to look at me with an enquiring eye questioning me as to what I want it to do and how it can please me. It is pleasing to know that my successor as Secretary, Mrs Carolyn Muirhead, is equally enthusiastic about retaining the working qualities in the show dog.

There are other clubs and societies which cater for enthusiasts of the breed on a regional basis. These bodies cover the South, Midlands and North together with Scotland, Wales and Northern Ireland. All except the Southern and Northern Societies have specific arrangements for the organisation of Field Trials. It is to be hoped that in the not too distant future these two societies will be able to extend their activities into the Field Trial world.

The last few years have seen a great increase in breed registrations at the Kennel Club. There has, in fact, been a minor population explosion. Entries at the Shows, especially the Championship Shows, have increased by some sixty per cent and the Field Trial Stakes are always over-subscribed. There are many new faces in the breed and a high proportion do not stay the course. There is no quick and easy short cut to the end of a carefully planned and successful breeding programme. It will take a lifetime of hard work and devotion.

The established Field Trial judges tell me that they are concerned at the lower standard of work in the field and it is certain that there is a great deal to be desired in the quality and type of the present day show Springer.

2 The Kennel Club Standard for the Breed

The Spaniel Club was founded in 1885 and the Standards for the different varieties of Spaniels were drawn up and submitted to the Kennel Club for approval.

The Kennel Club now issues a Standard of Points for all registered breeds and a knowledge of the Breed Standard is essential if you wish to select an English Springer for breeding purposes as this initial purchase will in all probability be the foundation of your kennel.

It is important to note that those responsible for drawing up the Breed Standard were all working enthusiasts and would fit into the current day description as 'Field Triallers'. Minor amendments have been recommended to and accepted by the Kennel Club since that time. Any amendments considered necessary are discussed by the Breed Clubs which then submit the proposed alterations to the Kennel Club. There the matter is discussed by the Breeds Standards Sub-Committee which is made up of a number of knowledgeable people from the canine world who recommend acceptance to the Executive Committee of the Kennel Club or request the Breed Clubs to give further thought to the changes proposed. It says much for the clarity of thinking and the wisdom of those who drew up the original Standard; that very few amendments have been made or thought to be necessary over a long period of time. It should always be remembered that the dog should fit the Standard and never should the Standard be made to fit the dog. This is what worries me when I hear people talking about 'the modern Springer'—is this a new breed they are developing?

The following is the only recognised Standard for the Breed:

CHARACTERISTICS: The English Springer is the oldest of our sporting gundogs and the tap-root from which all of our sporting land spaniels (Clumbers excepted) have been evolved. It was originally used for the purpose of finding and springing game for the net, falcon, or greyhound, but at the present time it is used entirely to find, flush and retrieve game for the gun. The breed is of ancient and pure origin, and should be kept as such.

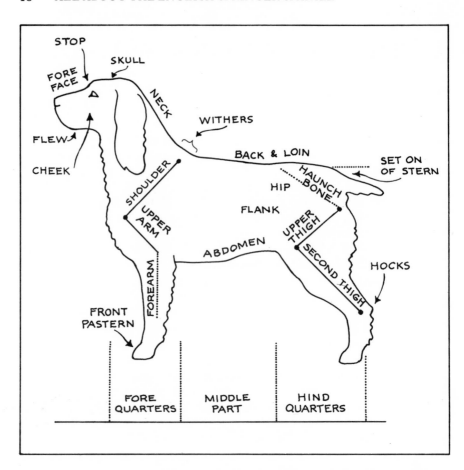

Fig. 1   The Points of the English Springer Spaniel

GENERAL APPEARANCE: The general appearance of the modern Springer is that of a symmetrical, compact, strong, upstanding, merry, and active dog, built for endurance and activity. He is the highest on the leg and raciest in build of all British land Spaniels.

Head and Skull: The skull should be of medium length and fairly broad and slightly rounded, rising from the foreface, making a brow or stop, divided by a fluting between the eyes gradually dying away along the forehead towards the occiput bone, which should not be peaked. The cheeks should be flat, that is not rounded or full. The foreface should be of proportionate length to the skull, fairly broad and deep without being coarse, well chiselled below the eyes, fairly deep and square in flew, but not exaggerated to such an extent as would interfere with comfort when retrieving. Nostrils well developed.

Eyes: The eyes should be neither too full nor too small but of medium size, not prominent nor sunken but well set in (not showing haw) of an alert, kind expression. A mouse-like eye without expression is objectionable, as also is a light eye. The colour should be dark hazel.

Ears: The ears should be lobular in shape, set close to the head, of good length and width, but not exaggerated. The correct set should be in a line with the eye.

Mouth: The jaws should be strong, with a perfect regular and complete scissor bite, i.e., the upper teeth closely overlapping the lower teeth and set square to the jaws.

Neck: The neck should be strong and muscular, of nice length and free from throatiness, well set in the shoulders, nicely arched and tapering towards the head—this giving great activity and speed. A ewe neck is objectionable.

Forequarters: The forelegs should be straight and nicely feathered, elbows set well to body and with proportionate substance to carry the body, strong flexible pasterns.

Body: The body should be strong and of proportionate length, neither too long nor too short, the chest deep and well developed with plenty of heart and lung room, well sprung ribs, loins muscular and strong with slight arch and well coupled, thighs broad and muscular and well developed.

Hindquarters: The hindlegs should be well let down from hip to hocks. Stifles and hocks moderately bent, inclining neither inwards nor outwards. Coarseness of hocks objectionable.

Feet: Feet tight, compact, and well rounded with strong full pads.

Gait: The Springer's gait is strictly his own. His forelegs should swing straight forward from the shoulder, throwing the feet well forward in an easy and free manner. His hocks should drive well under his body, following in a line with his forelegs. At slow movements many Springers have a pacing stride typical of the breed.

Tail: The stern should be low and never carried above the level of the back, well feathered and with a lively action.

Coat: The coat should be close, straight and weather resisting without being coarse.

Colour: Any recognised Land Spaniel colour is acceptable, but liver and white, black and white, or either of these colours with tan markings preferred.

Weight and Size: The approximate height should be 20 inches. The approximate weight should be 50 lb.

Note: Male animals should have two apparently normal testicles fully descended into the scrotum.

The Standard is comparatively easy to follow but there is a Scale of Points for judging which is complimentary to the written description.

Positive Points

Head and Jaws 10
Eyes 5
Ears 5
Neck 10
Body 20
Forelegs 10
Hindlegs..10
Feet 10
Stern 10
Coat and Feathers.................................10

Total Positive Points   =   100

The Standard explained

I think it worth while to add a few comments and some explanation to certain parts of the Standard.

Head and Skull: A skull should never be narrow, flat or domed. Lack of fluting between the eyes makes for a very plain head lacking in character and quality. The same can be said of lack of chiselling below the eyes and the rounded cheeks so common today. The true characteristic head of the English Springer was so apparent in most of the Ranscombe and Higham blood lines. A more recent example of a lovely head was Mr Ted Anderson's Dark Ranger of Crosslane.

Fig. 2   The Head (a) heavy, coarse skull (b) snipey head (c) well shaped head

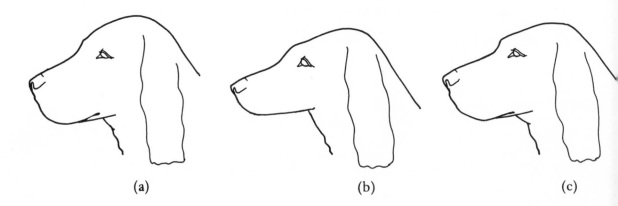

(a)   (b)   (c)

Eyes: Obviously the shape, colour and setting of the eye adds character to the dog. It should indicate an alert enquiring brain and give a kind expression. Loose eye rims exposing a great deal of haw expose the eye to damage when the dog is working in thick cover.

Ears: An ear that is too long will be a handicap to the working dog and if set too low tends more to the head of the Cocker Spaniel.

Mouth: The bite is most important and under no circumstance should dogs with mouth defects be used for breeding purposes. It is a fault that is difficult to eradicate and will recur in future generations for many years. Remember that this is a working dog and a proper jaw and tooth formation is essential for the retrieving of game.

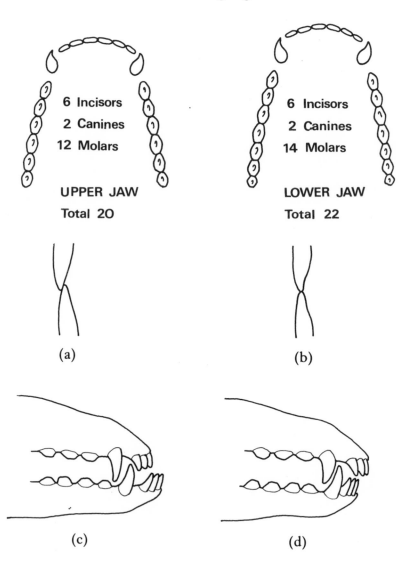

6 Incisors
2 Canines
12 Molars

UPPER JAW
Total 20

6 Incisors
2 Canines
14 Molars

LOWER JAW
Total 22

(a)

(b)

(c)

(d)

Fig. 3 Mouth and Teeth (a) correct scissor bite (b) even bite (c) undershot mouth (d) overshot mouth

Neck: A good reach of neck with good muscle is essential for the picking up of game which needs to be carried free of the ground. A lot of loose skin, called throatiness, detracts from the clean outline of the neck and can be a possible area of damage when working in dense briars.

Forequarters: The following diagram explains much of what the Standard infers:

Body: The body should be built so as to give the dog the stamina necessary for a hard day's work. A well developed rib cage with depth of brisket gives plenty of heart room. Strong, muscular loins, upper and second thighs are essential to give the dog drive, quick movement and spring.

Fig. 4 Front Action (a) splayed front (b) straight front (c) out at shoulders (d) well up on pastern (e) weak pastern (f) good lay back allows free action (g) bad lay back impedes free action (h) well laid shoulder (i) straight shoulder

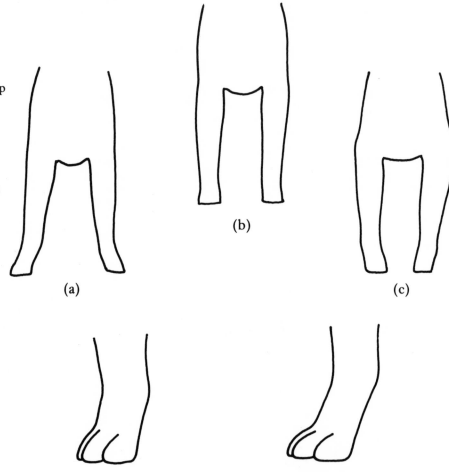

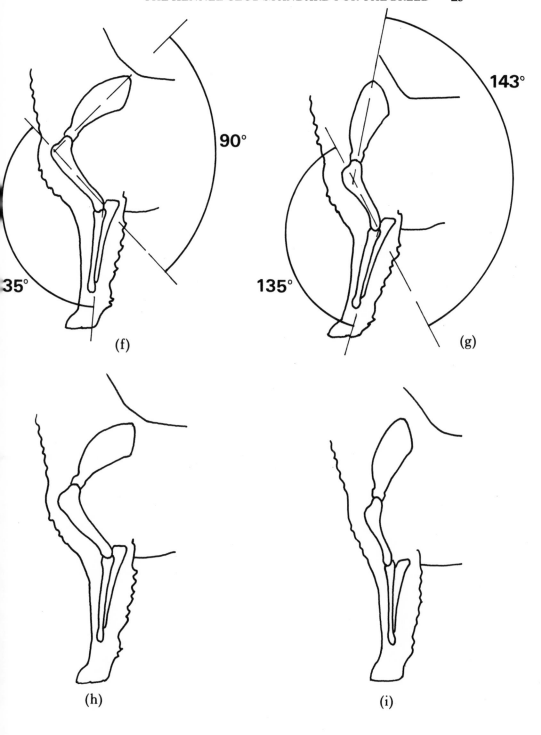

(f)

(g)

(h)

(i)

Hindquarters: Correct formation is needed for working ability and gives proper driving force from behind. There is, of course, the general ugliness of malformation.

Fig. 5   Back Action (a) well bent stifle aids propulsion (b) too straight a stifle impedes propulsion (c) bow hocked (d) good back legs (e) cow hocked

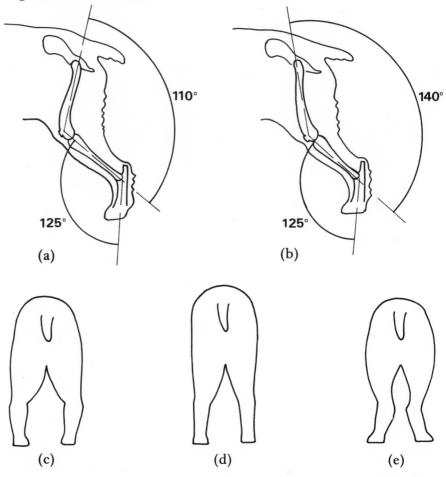

Feet: A loose foot becomes sore and is much more likely to be damaged by thorns.

Fig. 6   (a) well-rounded foot (b) hare foot (c) splayed foot

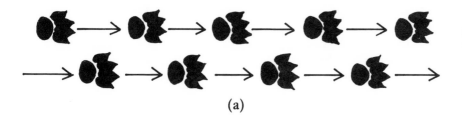

Fig. 7   (a) good gait (b) mincing gait or plaiting

(a)

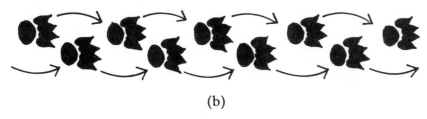

(b)

Gait: True Springer movement is a joy to watch—it appears to be so free and effortless. The hackney action is quite wrong. There should be no roll as this, whilst very marked in the present day strains, is quite foreign to the breed. The front action should not be paddling or hackney. The paddling action usually happens as a result of the dog being short in upper arm.

Tail: A tail that is carried above the level of the body is most objectionable. The lively action is a characteristic of the breed and an indication to the handler when game is about to be flushed from cover. There is a marked tendency today in the show world to dock tails far too short. This spoils the balance of the dog as a whole and accounts to some extent for the absence of proper tail action.

Coat: Prior to the 1934 revision of the Breed Standard a wavy coat was allowed. Some people are emphatic that a wavy coat produces a dense undercoat which of course will resist rain, water and briars. Personally, I find a wavy coat unattractive and have found it possible to have a straight coat that is also resistant to climate and undergrowth. Careful selection of blood lines can be very helpful. Generally a coarse wavy coat lacks a good undercoat.

Colour: Although I started with liver and white Springers I now lean heavily towards the black and whites. On the whole I find a kinder eye and expression coupled with better coats. One important advantage is that the black and white coat does not bleach in the summer. Both colours with tan markings are most attractive.

Weight and Size: Many show Springers are now well up to size and, conversely, there are some very small Field Trial dogs being worked. On the whole the Springer is required to work in cover and a large dog tends to jump over rather than work through. It could be that mere size makes it physically impossible for the dog to get underneath. A dog should stand approximately 20 inches at the shoulder for either sex. As far as weight is concerned, it must be consistent with an active life. The dog needs to be well covered but muscle is required—not fat.

One must always look at the overall picture and try not to be biased towards a particular or minor aspect of the Standard. In the end one is looking for good general conformation and movement. Always remember that the English Springer is a dog that should be built for work and that the original Standard was laid down by the shooting fraternity. It would be well at this point to put some emphasis on conformation and movement. Conformation is defined as a particular form, shape or structure or adaptation.

It does not refer to condition, fitness or carriage of the animal. Nor does it refer to the temperament. The Standard states that the English Springer is a symmetrical, compact, strong, upstanding, merry and active dog, built for endurance and activity. He should have a back of medium length, neither too short nor too long. All this refers to form, shape or structure and should present a mental picture of the animal. A dog which is over short in couplings cannot turn at speed which he needs to do when carrying out his purpose as a gundog. This is not meant to imply that he should be short in back and long in couplings, or vice versa.

In outline the animal should have a strong, muscular neck of nice length. This is necessary when carrying a heavy retrieve such as a 12 lb hare. The neck should fit into sloping shoulders.

An upright shoulder in any animal reduces the action of the foreleg and shortens the stride. An upright shoulder usually goes with a short upper arm and produces a paddling front action with the forelegs plaiting. It prevents the animal from extending properly in striding front action.

Working back from the shoulder the body should be deep with plenty of heart room, remembering that a working dog is required to keep going for five or six hours and may cover 20 miles or more depending on the terrain. Ribs should be well sprung but should not be so great that they impede the action of the forelegs. Loins should be muscular and strong with a slight arch, and well coupled. Overweight in this area considerably reduces the efficient.

The main power house is in the hindquarters. They should be muscular and in hard condition. The stifle should be moderately bent. Straight stifles restrict the movement whilst too great an angle leads to weakness, by being too flexible. Hocks are of vital importance and cow hocks are probably the most common and noticeable fault. This produces a twisting movement in the hind leg and the animal may even plait. Bow or sickle hocks prevent the weight dropping through the muscles and bone of the leg so causing the dog to roll. This rolling movement also occurs when the elbows are set too far out. There is a tendency today for animals to be coarse in hock, this leads to the erroneous assumption that heavy and coarse bone is correct, this is not so as a working animal needs strong flexible bone without unnecessary weight.

Unfortunately the present type of working dog strays from the Standard just as much as the present day show dog. This is because they have over emphasised the performance of the dog as against a certain amount of overall balance. The need for speed has resulted in a dog which is too long in couplings. You may have noticed from watching the parade of runners prior to the race that 'the horse which wins the Derby is not necessarily a perfect example of conformation'. There is a need for both sides to aim for the perfect specimen.

Feet are all important in a working breed. They should be very compact and deep. Everyone knows that flat feet tire more easily and are more prone to accidents during work.

The eyes should not show any sign of haw or any other deformity which would allow a foreign body to enter the eye. The skull should have a fluting through the stop to the top of the head. It is well known that animals with a hound formation in the skull are much more obstinate to train. There should also be considerable chiselling around the eyes. The cheeks should be flat and the flews not too square as this interferes with a clean retrieve. Nostrils should be well developed and not pinched, as the dog needs all the scent buds it can have. It is essential that the bite be of a tight scissor type.

The tail should be of the utmost importance in a working breed and should never be docked by more than the removal of 3/5ths. It is impossible to know what your dog means when it is working if it does not have sufficient tail to indicate its intentions or the type of game it has winded. The carriage is all important and should be set below the level of the back. The feathering should not be shaved off, only tidied up for the show ring. This is protection in heavy, thick and punishing cover.

The ideal height is approximately 20 inches for either sex, dogs over this height are more suited to work as non-slip retrievers than the true work of the Spaniel which is why the height was reduced by one inch in the 1920s.

3 The Show Springer

I hope that at the beginning of this book I have made it clear that in the early days of the breed the emphasis was on work and very little interest was to be found for shows. The very early Springers were, of course, something of a mixed bag. The off-spring of one breed sometimes being registered as a Springer and the off-spring of a Springer being included in another breed register. Examples of this are to be found in Guy of Gerewyn (son of a Welsh Springer) registered as a Springer whilst a daughter of a famous Springer Beechgrove Will was registered as a Field Spaniel. It seems that cross-breds and Setters and some of the old Norfolk Spaniels all acquired labels as Springers.

It was not until 1902 that the Kennel Club set up a separate Register for English Springers and offered a class especially for the breed at their Show in 1903. By 1906 Mr Winton Smith's liver and white dog Beechgrove Will had become the first champion Springer dog and Mr Harry Jones' Fansom the first champion bitch. There were few enthusiasts for shows and few show dogs. The chief exhibitors around that time were Mr W. Arkwright, Mr H. Jones, Mr I. Sharpe, Mr C. Watts, Mr F. Winton Smith and Sir Hugo Fitz-Herbert. Little progress was made before 1914 and then the First World War was with us and it was not until after 1918 and the end of the War that registrations began to show any marked increase. This increase continued until 1925 when there was a slight decline for a number of years. I have included a table at the end of this book which shows the variation and yet it appears that during periods of lower registrations the popularity of the breed as working dogs increased considerably, and there was no lack of entries for Field Trial events and in Chapter 4 I will mention some famous Springers of that time. Notable Stud dogs of the era were Ch. Rivington Sam, Ch. Flint of Avendale, Ch. Springbok of Ware, Ch. Denne Duke and Ch. Little Brand.

In the 1920s many of the Championship Shows began to get organised again but only two shows classified English Springers at the beginning of this period. In October 1920 classes were available at the Scottish Kennel Club Show held in Edinburgh where the dog C.C. winner was Mr D. McDonald's Little Brand and the bitch C.C. went to Mr L. Turton Prices' Horsford Honeybell. Later in the same year at

Crystal Palace the Kennel Club Show provided classes and once again Mr McDonald won the Challenge Certificates; the dog with Little Brand and the bitch with Little Sunray. Over the next four or five years shows expanded rapidly and English Springers were classified at over a dozen Championship Shows. The winning dogs around this time were Mr Haley's Monas Queen, Mr H. S. Lloyd's Nutbrook Boy, Mr D. McDonald's Ch. Linwhinny Crowle, Mr. D. Shaw's Rex of Auchwear, Mr Harold Owen's Shellback Dolphin, Mr T. Ford Lowe's Worthen Surprise and Worthen Suspense. Over this period the prefixes Beauchief, Marmiom, Solway, Shotton and of Ware were very prominent. So many of these prefixes can be found in the pedigrees of present day Springers that some little comment about them as individuals may well be of interest to those who take an interest in the history of the breed.

Beauchief is the prefix of Mr Frank Warner Hill who must know more about Springers than anyone else alive today. He is world renowned as a judge of many breeds but I would imagine that gundogs were always his first love, especially the Springer. His first and foundation bitch was registered as Beauchief Lady Barbara and from her first litter sired by Int. Ch. Jambok of Ware she added Beauchief Nicholas and Beauchief Major to the kennel. Some time later Mr Hill bought a little working bitch whose pedigree was made up mostly of kennel names only but in the part of Derbyshire where she was bought pedigrees, if not on paper, were very definite and accurate in the minds of the keepers and owners. From this bitch Mr Hill produced Ch. Beauchief Bonnetta who in turn was dam to his most famous dog Ch. Beauchief Benefactor. This dog's special claim to fame is due to the fact that he

Mr F. Warner Hill's Ch. Beauchief Benefactor.

was the first British bred and owned Springer to win the Best in Show award at a General Championship Show.

Marmion owned by the Hon. George Scott. His Ch. Marmion of Marmion appears in so many winning pedigrees. Another well known winner was Ch. Constance of Marmion.

Of Solway suffix was owned by Mr R. Grierson who was active in the breed in the 1930s. His best winning year was in fact 1930 when he won fourteen C.C.s with Champions Administrator of Solway, Advert of Solway, Lovebird of Solway and Follow Through of Solway. Half-way through the decade his Ch. Winning Number of Solway was at the top of the awards, as also was Ch. Dry Toast.

Of Ware the suffix of the Internationally famous Wizard of Ware, the late Mr H. S. Lloyd. To many present day exhibitors, Mr Lloyd's name is linked with Cocker Spaniels but in the 1920s he owned three Springer Champions—Springbok of Ware, Jambok of Ware and Jamson of Ware. Mr Lloyd was Chairman of the English Springer Spaniel Club for a number of years and it was under his Chairmanship that I became Honorary Secretary to the Club and so remained for some twenty-five years. Ch. Springbok of Ware was exported to the States where he joined Mr Chevrier's Avondale Kennels.

Shotton was owned by Mr Michael Withers although the kennel was managed by Mrs Gwen Broadley. The dogs were highly successful in the show ring and Int. Ch. Showman of Shotton had considerable influence on the breed but eventually went to the States. Ch. Jess of Shelcot and Ch. Beauchief Barham were also in his kennel. The Shotton suffix has a special meaning for me because it was Mr Withers who gave me my first Springer as a wedding present in 1944. For some years before that I had kept Cocker Spaniels buying one or two from Mr A. B. Nicolson whose Glenbervie prefix was also known in Springers and Whippets.

It is of course, so difficult to mention all the earlier dogs and owners by name but all have had their part to play even in a small way in the development of the breed. I would just like to mention two more kennels in some detail because their owners have played a very special part in the mid 1900s to keep alive the working side. In the early days of shows, a dog could only become a Champion after winning his three C.C.s under three different judges and then gaining a qualifier in the field. Many of us regret the day when in the 1950s the Kennel Club decided to introduce the status of Show Champion. In other words there could now be a Show Champion and a Field Trial Champion which meant that the working qualification need not be obtained. The title of Champion was retained for award to the Show Champions that qualified in the field. For several years now, only a few Springers have made full Champion status and I believe that my own Ch. Larkstoke

Grisette is the only black and white full champion bitch in the country today. I feel, therefore, that the kennels which have stood out for the working qualities in the not so distant past should be given a little more space.

Higham prefix was owned by the late Miss C. M. Francis. A great horsewoman and rider to hounds she was convinced that the working qualities of the Springer should be maintained and for this purpose she worked towards the dual purpose dog. Her best known dogs were Ch. Higham Topsy, Ch. Higham Teal and Ch. Higham Tom Tit. The latter was sold to Mrs Selby-Lowndes, later to be Lady Lambe. A nice looking working dog from this kennel called Higham Ted did some winning at Shows and at Field Trials. I introduced this blood line into my own kennel and achieved much quality, good temperament and sound working ability. I believe that only Mr Alfred Fowle (Whitebrook) and myself still retain any of this excellent blood line. Miss Francis served for many years as Chairman and finally as President of the English Springer Spaniel Club. A Founder Member of the English Springer Spaniel Club, she was held in high esteem by all who knew her as a judge of Shows and Field Trials and as a person with great knowledge of the Springer. I felt privileged to be the recipient under the terms of her Will of all her dog papers and records.

Ranscombe was the suffix of Miss Morland Hooper another Founder Member of the English Springer Spaniel Club and its Field Trial Secretary for some sixteen years. Miss Hooper was naturally a great

Reverie of Ranscombe owned by the late Miss D. Morland Hooper.

supporter of the working side and she ran her dogs at Trials. She won awards at the Kennel Club Show in 1920 with Ranger of Ranscombe. Many winners of the 'R' group came along including Rollick, Reipple, Roam, Ramp and Rascal. Very knowledgeable in the breed and its early days, it was really Miss Hooper and Miss Francis who convinced me that there was so much to be gained from training and working a dog.

Other prefixes and suffixes that need a brief mention are *of Harting* (Lt. Col. F. Carrell) Dual Ch. Thoughtful of Harting was one of the few Dual Champions ever bred and I doubt very much that we shall ever see any more in Springers.

Mr S. H. Till owns the *Roundwood* prefix and his Ch. Roundwood Lass (descended from Ch. Rufton Recorder) won nearly thirty Challenge Certificates. *Rufton* was owned by Mr R. Cornthwaite and his Ch. Rufton Recorder was an influence on the breed here before he was sent across the Atlantic. Mr. A. McNab Chassels owned the *Inveresk* prefix and his Ch. Inveresk Chancellor was a well known dog that was exported to Canada where he became a Triple International Champion. For many years Mr McNab Chassels was Convenor of the Scottish Kennel Club.

The *Laverstoke* prefix was owned by Lady Portal who bred two well known champion dogs—Laverstoke Pepper and Laverstoke Pattern. Other winning dogs included Laverstoke Pancake and Laverstoke Pedro.

Mr George Taylor practised as a chemist and was a great character with dogs carrying his *Carnfield* prefix. Carnfield Albie Legione, Carnfield Chick, Carnfield Field Marshall and Carnfield Florrie are all names that bring back memories of George Taylor and his waxed Kaiser moustache. A bitch from this kennel was purchased by Mr D. T. Hannah and became the foundation of the *Stokeley* Springers.

The *Boghurst* prefix was winning in the early 1920s when Major H. E. C. Doyne-Ditmas was showing Boghurst Carlo and Boghurst Rover. A Champion dog carrying this prefix—Boghurst Bristle—was owned by Mr McNab Chassels. Mr Reg Kelland was a founder member and Secretary, Chairman and President of the English Springer Spaniel Club who owned the *Nobel* prefix. A great authority on the breed he bred his own dogs and competed successfully at Shows and Field Trials. Until his death he lived fairly close to us first at Dunnington and then at nearby Bidford-on-Avon. I remember his first visit to us on a Sunday afternoon when there was quite a lot of snow on the ground. We were then living in a somewhat isolated house in the Cotswolds near Chipping Campden and I do not really think he was prepared for the conditions having travelled up from the milder climate of the Avon Valley. He had come to ask me whether I would be Secretary of the English Springer Spaniel Club. He was, of course, one of the great personalities of the breed and a firm and forthright official

Ch. Carnfield Chrystabelle owned by the late Mr G. A. Taylor.

of the Club. Towards the end of this early period, that is to say the early 1940s two other dogs need mention for they had considerable influence on the breed. One was Mr Tom Naseby's Ch. Pleasant Peter and Mr G. R. Musgrave's Peter's Benefactor. Benefactor was a son of Pleasant Peter and won several hundred awards but he could not gain his title as the Championship Shows had not yet restarted after the Second World War.

My own Springer, registered as Pixie of Larkstoke, came to me in 1944 and whilst I knew a number of the people and dogs I have mentioned, a great many were of course, nothing more than names to me but I made it my business to find out about them from people such as Donald MacDonald, 'Bert' Lloyd, Reg Kelland, Miss Francis and others and I have always maintained a scrap-book with photographs of past and present dogs. My entry into the breed was at the end of the Second World War during which time no Championship Shows had been held although the smaller Societies had carried on with Sanction Shows and other events. The English Springer Spaniel Club held its first post-war Championship Show at Reading in 1946 and it received an entry which to the best of my knowledge has never been bettered. Mr Ernest Trimble was the judge and he awarded the dog C.C. to Whaddon Chase Bonny Tom and the bitch C.C. to Sandylands Sherry. The previous year the newly formed Midland English Springer Spaniel Society had put on its first Open Show for the breed and this also received a large entry to be judged by Mr A. McNab Chassels. He awarded Best Dog and Best in Show to Mr G. A. Taylor's Carnfield Field Marshall and Best Bitch to Staitley Sunlight. After a break of several years owing to the War there was bound to be considerable discussion as to how the breed in the mid 1940s compared with stock being shown pre-war. It seems that on the whole the older and established authorities on the breed were disappointed with what they saw.

In July 1946 the Midland Society organised a second Open Show to be judged (with the sexes divided) by Mr W. East and Mr J. Gibson, and another excellent entry was recorded and the judges found their Best in Show in Mr Joe Braddon's Starshine of Ide whose pedigree included two early and well known dogs I have already mentioned. He was sired by Peter of Shotton and the dam was Ch. Jess of Shelcot. This was the beginning of a run of successes for Mr Braddon to be followed by a string of twenty-five C.Cs with Ch. Invader of Ide. The latter was Irish bred and purchased by Mr Braddon from Mr R. Cleland who was later to pilot his Grand Lodge to Championship status. At about the same time Mrs Gwen Broadley's Sandylands Kennel came to the fore and she was winning with Sandylands Starling, Showgirl, Shrubly, Shandy and Soubranie later owned by Mr E. Lumb Taylor. At roughly this time a new suffix appeared in the show catalogues. This was *Happeedaze* owned by Mr W. Rankin Hepplewhite who by the end of the 1940's had made up two Champions; Ch. Sprightly of Happeedaze and Ch. Solitaire of Happeedaze. The latter was a very nice quality bitch and one that I liked a lot. It was at roughly this time that many people were using a young stud dog Boxer of Bamhope who belonged to Mrs Mary Scott. This dog did a lot of winning in his early days but was not shown to any great extent after the age of about four years. He did, however, have a tremendous influence on the breed and I well remember some years ago trying to find an outcross that did not carry any Boxer of Bramhope blood and it was a very difficult task. The *Bramhope* kennel went on to produce a great many winners including Ch. Belarosa of Bramhope and Ch. Bathsheba of Bramhope. The main influence of the Bramhope prefix will have been exerted by the sons of Boxer who were all used extensively at stud—Ch. Alexander of

Stubham, Ch. Peter of Lortonfell and Ch. Studley Major. Mrs Scott later imported a dog from Mrs R. Gilman Smith in the States and I remember her telling me that she felt she ought to do something to provide an outcross in the breed after the use that had been made of Boxer. The dog that came across was a liver and white dog that had already gained his Championship status, Am. Ch. Melilotus Shooting Star. I think this must have been a disappointment for Mary Scott because he never won well in this country and was not used at stud to any extent. Sometime later another American dog, a black and white called Dr Primrose stayed in this country for a time en route to Australia. Once again he did little winning and was not widely accepted as an alternative stud. Quite frankly I do not feel that either of these dogs was good enough for what was wanted in the country at the time. Years earlier our best stock, for instance Int. Ch. Showman of Shotton, had gone out to the States to help form the backbone of the breed over there. We needed something equally good back again in return but all credit must go to Mary Scott for seeing the need and doing her best to meet it.

Lady Lambe, formerly Mrs Selby-Lowndes, was winning C.C.s with dogs carrying her well known *Whaddon Chase* prefix. At this time Whaddon Chase Bonny Tom, Whaddon Chase Snipe, and Waddon Chase Titch, Whaddon Chase Bracken and Whaddon Chase Prince were winning well. A number of Lady Lambe's exhibits were black and white and from this time on we find them becoming increasingly popular.

Lady Lambe's Ch. Whaddon Chase Bonny Tom.

Whaddon Chase Bonny Tom sired a puppy out of a bitch called Clintonhouse Elizabeth and this gave Mr D. C. Hannah his first Champion in Stokeley Bonny Boy. The kennel went on to produce Stokeley Gay Boy, Stokeley Lucky, Stokeley Sea Sprite, Stokeley Sea Princess and many other winners. At his Nottinghamshire home Mr Hannah had a well organised rabbit pen set up in an old quarry and he was never happier than when he was able to get out training his dogs. In later life he changed his interest completely to the field trial world and we very seldom saw him at a show again. He had already bred some winners in field trials when he died suddenly. For many years he was Chairman of the Midland Society. The late 1940s also saw prize cards and C.C.s going to the *Winch* kennel of Mrs G. Crawford and Winch Agate. This small kennel had always produced stock of fine quality and lovely typical Springer heads. Light of Ashleigh owned by Mr A. B. Nicolson and Peter of Lortonfell owned by Mr J. C. Hanning saw out the end of the 1940s. Both were to become well known Champions in the breed.

Although the early part of the 1950s saw many of the older prefixes in the winning line up, the breed was beginning to attract newcomers. Lady Lambe and Mrs Broadley continued to win, Mrs Broadley with a new one called Castlecary Cameronian that she made up quickly and sold to the States. Mr R. A. Morgan started his championship run with his own Leymor Recorder and Birkdale Beggarmaid that he handled for Dr Aubrey Ireland. Mr Ernest Froggatt also began a championship show run with a black and white called Bramhope Recorder, eventually to be a full champion, and this was the beginning of a successful show career for Ernest and the Moorcliff Kennels. Mr J. Bolton started to show his Tillan Toddy who later collected a total of fifteen C.C.s. This was a very nice bitch and one I well remember. At this time I was showing my Larkstoke Sugar Candy who collected at least nine reserve C.C.s behind Tillan Toddy. By the time Tillan Toddy had been withdrawn I had lost my bitch following a caesarean operation. She had won two C.C.s and qualified in the field and to meet Toddy on so many occasions did prove a little disappointing.

In 1951 the late famous Alexander of Stubham won his first two C.C.s for his owner Mrs F. Oughtred Till. Later 'Alex' went on to win a total of twenty-two C.C.s and to join his sire Boxer of Bramhope as one of the leading stud dogs in the breed. Mr Sandy Davies who had previously been winning with his Colmaris Toreador now produced Clintonhouse George and made him into a champion by winning all three C.C.s in 1952. The following year Invader of Ide, Alexander of Stubham and Clintonhouse George, all champions in the breed, continued to be the strongest winners. A new dog, Studley Major owned by Mrs M. Smithson collected three tickets and his title in 1953 and three new bitches were made up—Wollburn Wallflower owned by Mr A. B. Nicolson, Dinah of Stubham owned by Mr R. Grant and Colmaris Contessa owned by Mr Sandy Davies. Whaddon Chase Grouse, Romance and Swift were all regularly in the final line up.

The mid 1950s saw competition for top awards between Clintonhouse George, Alexander of Stubham and Peter of Lortonfell. Another Studley dog entered the field named Studley Brave Buccaneer and eventually gained his championship status. In bitches Ch. Colmaris Contessa led the field and Mrs Harold Frankish produced another champion in Beanmore Camdin Greta. By this time two leading dogs were dead, Ch. Peter of Lortonfell and Ch. Clintonhouse George. Then Print of Ardrick, later to become an International Champion, took top place in the breed at Crufts in 1958. In dogs the later 1950s saw a fairly even distribution of the C.C.s with the better known winners being Stokeley Sea Sprite, Stokeley Sea Princess, Mr Donald Campbell's Inverruel Raider and Mr R. G. Thomas' Conquest of Clyne and another new one in Mr E. E. A. Stevenson's Bonaventure of Bramhope.

It was in 1958 that the Kennel Club approved the new title of Show Champion and among the first dogs entitled to use the new prefix were Bonaventure of Bramhope, Stokeley Sea Sprite, Stokeley Sea Princess, Colmaris Nice Fella, Colmaris Ranger, Beauvallet of Crosslane, Brandyhole Berry Brown, Vanity Fair of Stubham, Studley Debutante, Sandylands Susanna and Glencora County Maid.

Mowgrain Mr Chips owned by Mrs J. Midgley was already a champion by 1957 when he was the leading dog. A very nice bitch, Northdown Donna, owned by Mr W. Manin and Mrs Frances Sherwood won her three Certificates and at this time Miss Judith Robinson was showing her Onyx of Stubham and winning two certificates with her. This was perhaps the beginning of the success story for Judith Robinson (later to become Judith Hancock) and her *Hawkhill* prefix. For a number of years Judith had been working with Mrs Oughtred Till and was well acquainted with the Stubham stock. In the latter part of this decade competition in bitches was strong and very few new faces were to be seen among the certificate winners.

There were, of course, a great many people showing good and promising youngsters that never reached the top and a few that fell by the wayside. Over the first fifty to sixty years of the development of the Show Springer I have restricted my comment to the well known prefixes for up to this time, there was not much change in the number of exhibitors the breed attracted. Once you were committed you stayed but now I think we have changed. As we enter the period which will bring us up to current time we shall find some of the people I have mentioned as being in the background coming to the fore and whilst the breed has maintained a committed nucleus of enthusiasts there is much more

Sh. Ch. Hawkhill
Connaught owned
by Mrs J. A.
Hancock and Mr J.
P. Cudworth.

'coming and going' in the show ring today. I, of course, believe that this
is an indication of the times we now live in when attitudes have certainly
changed. Maybe dogs are now exhibited for different reasons and the
need to win has become that much more important. At the same time I
receive an increasing number of enquiries for Springer puppies and their
popularity for work and show has certainly increased. Happily one can
say that the increased popularity is not tremendous for I would not like
to see the breed pass through the same stages as say Boxers, Cockers and
currently Irish Setters. I have already mentioned Mrs Hancock (formerly
Miss Judith Robinson) and I think it would be true to say that the late
60s and most of the 70s have been dominated by the Hawkhill prefix. In
partnership with Mr Jimmy Cudworth, Judith steered show champion
Hawkhill Connaught to a position that no other English Springer has
attained in the Show world. In the Dog of the Year Competition he
shared top award in 1972 and was top dog in 1973. I think he won just
over fifty challenge certificates and some sixteen Gundog Groups at the
General Championship Shows. Other Hawkhill dogs of note in this
period were Finlandia, Happy Memory, Wishful Thinking handled by

Judith and Jimmy and many others including Show Champions H. Royal Palace, Hello Dolly, Finlandia and other owners such as Sh. Ch. Hawkhill Derby Daydream, Sh. Ch. Hawkhill St. Pauli Girl of Moorcliff, Hawkhill Harmonius; Hawkhill Prince Consort of Moorcliff. Mr Ernest Froggatt was there most of the time. Two of his dogs carrying the Moorcliff prefix have just been mentioned and he had a long run of successful Champions, including Moorcliff Dougal of Truelindale. Mrs Sherwood, Mr Manin and Mrs Hannah were still there notching up the wins with Sh. Ch. Woodbay Dianes Dilly, Sh. Ch. Woodbay Don Derry and Sh. Ch. Stokeley Son of Laddie. Mrs Ellen Dobson was there with Ch. Tyneview Margaret to be followed by many notable dogs carrying her Teesview prefix such as Ch. Teesview Titus and Ch. Teesview Tarmac, Sh. Ch. Teesview Twister and that well known bitch Sh. Ch. Teesview Pandora of Truelindale. The owner of the *Truelindale* prefix is Miss M. Alder and the reader will have noted already that Miss Alder had bred a few champions for other people. Mrs B. Carstairs has won C.C.s with her Whitemoor prefix notably Sh. Ch. Whitemoor Lady Diane, Sh. Ch. Whitemoor Idle Chat and Sh, Ch. Whitemoor Idle Rich.

Ch. Tyneview Margaret owned by Mrs Ellen Dobson.

Ch. Larkstoke
Grisette bred and
owned by the
author.

I had made up my Larkstoke Ptarmigan and Larkstoke Grisette and won a lot of prizes and Working Test events with Larkstoke Willywicket.

Mrs J. Oakey (Eydon), Mrs D. George (Mortondawn), Mrs L. Lyons (Kylemore), Mrs D. Bury with her Sh. Ch. Hildary Roast Chesnut, Mr E. Chadburn with Sh. Ch. Trand Bren Ragapple, Mrs J. Cule with Sh. Ch. Mastermind of Mordax, Mr R. Jackson with Sh. Ch. Moorcliff Sunnymaid, Mr and Mrs Norman with Sh. Ch. St. Trillos Grecian Girl and Mrs Lillie with Sh. Ch. Barlochan Bellringer have all done a credible amount of winning.

Mr and Mrs D. Miller, now Secretary and Treasurer of the Southern English Springer Spaniel Society, came into the breed from Alsatians and in addition to building the Society into a flourishing concern have been very successful in the show ring with their *Feorlig* prefix and made up their first Show Champion in Feorlig Beautiful Memory. Many newcomers to the breed in the South of England are now holding stock from this kennel.

I mentioned earlier the increase in popularity of the black and white Springer and although earlier exhibitors of the breed such as Miss Francis and Lady Lambe always had this colour in their kennels, it is largely due to the efforts of Mrs Jean Taylor that the colour has been brought to the top of the winning line and her *Cleavehill* prefix is so well known. Sh. Ch. Cleavehill Corn Dolly was her first to be made up to be followed by Cleavehill Tarton Arrow, Islay Lass and others. Not to be

outdone in the family success, her husband Bill has made up two
Springers, Sh. Ch. Cleavehill Brigadier and Sh. Ch. Cleavehill Yankee
Clipper but he was not fully converted to the black and white system.

Another breeder who has fostered the black and white Springer is Mr
Colin Muirhead. In fact the whole family is involved and I am sure that
the *Shipden* prefix is in joint ownership. Their noted black and white was
Ch. Swallowtail of Shipden, a grand dog who proved a good sire and I
used him myself to produce my Larkstoke Avocet who has done very
well at Working Tests at the Spaniel Field Day. Another Champion from
the Shipden Kennel was Sh. Ch. Persimmon of Shipden and Int. Ch.
Sotherton Phantom of Shipden. Mr and Mrs B. G. Smith bred Phantom
together with another black and white Sh. Ch. Sotherton Sky Warrior.
Both were sired by one of the Muirheads' older dogs Kublai-Khan of
Shipden. The Muirheads, of course, have a wider interest in gundogs
and together with daughter Catherine are also showing Sussex and
Fields successfully. I was very pleased, when I retired as Secretary of the

A group of
Cleavehill Springers
owned by Mrs Jean
Taylor.

Ch. Swallowtail of Shipden owned by Mr and Mrs C. J. Muirhead.

English Springer Spaniel Club, that Carolyn Muirhead should be elected as my successor. As a family they have a sound knowledge of the breed and a belief that the show people must not be allowed to forget the working side.

I would not wish to end my comment on black and white Springers without another mention of Mr Alfred Fowle. He retains with me, most of what is left of Miss Francis' Higham blood lines and he is a regular and sporting exhibitor at most of the Championship Shows. Some few years back he made up a great quality bitch Sh. Ch. Sapphire of Shipden. Although Alfred Fowle may not always be winning he has usually got something useful in the kennel, good looking, with sense, working ability and grand temperament.

I have mentioned the Spaniel Field Day. Some years ago it was felt that there was a need for an event to which show people could take their dogs especially to gain a Qualifier other than at a Field Trial where quite often, not the right kind of attention was given to the procedure. Mr F. Oughtred Till of the Stubham prefix put the idea to the Kennel Club and approval was given subject to at least one Panel A judge being approved for the event. Mr and Mrs Till organised the initial event in 1966 and then the management of what became known as the Spaniel Field Day passed to Dr Peter Ferrer and then to his father, Mr Harold Ferrer. The whole event was under the general protection of the Midland English Springer Spaniel Society but was supported by the other English Springer Clubs and Societies together

Swiss Ch. Larkstoke Waxwing.

with a number of other Spaniels breeds. The Secretaries of the Midland Society, Mr and Mrs Jeffrey Backhouse have been in office for many years and so it was natural that when Mr Ferrer gave up his work with the Spaniel Field Day that they should take it over. It has gone from strength to strength and is highly successful. One could wish, however, for a higher percentage of qualifiers for English Springers, bearing in mind their numerical superiority. The Welsh Springers and Irish Water Spaniels at this event have certainly shown the English Springers that they can do the job as well, and sometimes better. It was a great pleasure to me to win Best Performance of the Day and First in the Advanced Test with my Larkstoke Willywicket. I treasured it far

Larkstoke Willywicket.

more than my Show prize cards. The Backhouses, like me, had Cockers before coming into Springers and their Majeba prefix is well known in the North. Jeff puts a lot of time into training his dogs and is no mean shot into the bargain. Sh. Ch. Majeba Mac and Sh. Ch. Majeba Meadowmint (the latter owned by Mr L. Antcliff), are two of their better known Springers. The efforts of people like Jeff and Margaret Backhouse are of immense value if we are to keep pressing home the need to maintain working instincts in the Show dog. Over the last five years it is sad to report that only two English Springers have achieved full Champion Status during which time some twenty-five Show Champions have been reported.

As always we need ground for field events and this is becoming increasingly difficult to obtain. The Spaniel Field Day has been extremely fortunate in that another Springer enthusiast, Mr Ted Anderson, has freely given his land at St Ives, Huntingdon, for so many events. Ted Anderson has been a popular Chairman of the English Springer Spaniel Club and is now our President. His best known winning Springer was Sh. Ch. Beauvallet of Crosslane and although the Andersons did not show a great deal in recent years there was always a useful Springer or two around the house. My husband was always very taken with Dark Ranger of Crosslane for she had a really wonderful and true Springer head. It was with much sadness that we sent our sympathy to Ted Anderson and his family when Mrs Anderson died so suddenly. As hostess to the Spaniel Field Day, and for the great service she did for the breed, she will be remembered for many a day.

For many years Mrs Jean Oakey of the *Eydon* prefix has been supporting the Shows and winning prizes at Championship Shows. Her first bitch was Field Trial bred and it was this bitch mated to one of Mr Hannah's Stokeley dogs that laid the foundation for her present Kennel.

This brings me to the leading dog of the moment Ch. Cliffhill Julius for he shares with my own Ch. Larkstoke Grisette the honour of occupying those two places on the list of Champions. Julius, owned by Mr and Mrs D. Sheppard, is a son of Ch. Teesview Titus and has had a good winning run. His progeny are winning up and down the country. Now as I close this chapter I realise that so many people have not been mentioned but it is a difficult task. Quite often it is the minor but regular winners who form the background and the staying power of a breed. There are the steady winners of today and I would mention exhibitors like Mrs Eteo, Mrs and Miss Wilson, Mr and Mrs Lillie, Miss Janet Shaw, Mr Phillip Green and numerous others. Sometimes I worry about the future and look at the general breeding pattern of the past, starting with Boxer of Bramhope and then going on to the 'use the top dog' syndrome and the pattern builds up from Ch. Alexander of Stubham (son of Boxer), down to Ch. Cliffhill Julius. Surely now again Mary Scott would be looking for that outcross?

What are they like these Springers? I think we should now be very seriously taking stock for over the past years we appear to have lost something of type, quality, temperament and working ability.

4 The Field Trial Springer

All must accept that the English Springer is a working breed and it might be said that appearance should not be the only criterion in assessing the dog. However, it is sometimes very difficult to reconcile the ideals and concepts of those who breed purely for work and those who breed purely for show. The show dogs of today are certainly larger and heavier than most of those that we see in the field and I would be inclined to agree that the size and weight of bone to be carried at work all day is excessive. On the purely working side there has been the tendency to produce a smaller and lighter Springer. However, there is working opinion that looks mattered very little so long as the dog did the job. To some extent I feel that there is lack of understanding and interpretation of the Standard particularly by the Show breeders who have for so long confused the terms 'short in couplings' with 'short in the back'. We need a dog that is short in couplings but a dog that is short in back cannot turn at speed. Before the divergence became too great blood lines such as Higham, Ranscombe, Stokeley and Northdown could produce dogs capable of winning at shows and in the field and here there was a sharing of the ancestry. When Miss Hooper of the Ranscombe prefix judged at Crufts she awarded both dog and bitch C.C.s to exhibits in the Field Trial Class and these were Ch. Higham Topsy and Ch. Stokeley Lucky. I think it is still true to say that Crufts and the English Springer Spaniel Club are the only two Shows to provide classes for Field Trial dogs and each year the number of entries has been getting progressively smaller.

I have, somewhat sadly, come to the conclusion that a point of no return has been reached, each side having exaggerated particular features in order to achieve a particular goal.

When we look at pedigrees of dogs in the early 1900s they all go back to the same strains and I would like to look at some of the blood lines in the same way as I dealt with the show blood lines of this early period.

Denne was the prefix of Mr C. C. Eversfield who lived at Denne Park at Horsham in Sussex. At the beginning of the 1900s he was winning at trials. His earlier dogs were registered as Fields but his famous dog was Velox Powder and this dog's pedigree could be traced back through the Aqualate stock to 1812. Velox Powder won his first trial in 1904, was

The late Miss D. Morland Hooper's Replica of Ranscombe.

never unplaced at the events he entered for the next eight years, and was, of course, a F.T. Champion.

Rivington, the prefix of Mr C. A. Phillips, was in competition at this time and the best known dog of this line was F.T. Ch. Rivington Sam. Undoubtedly this prefix had a tremendous influence on the working Springer.

Avendale was the prefix of the Duke of Hamilton and Brandon. His kennels were producing field trials winners that were in competition with the Denne and Rivington strains. A winning dog at this time was FT. Ch. Rex of Avendale and later that famous Dual Champion Flint of Avendale.

It was men such as Mr C. A. Phillips, Mr William Arkwright, Mr. C. C. Eversfield and a few others who did so much to establish the English Springer. Mr John Kent, first won at Field Trials in 1905 and his first F.T. Ch. was a Cocker Spaniel made up the following year. From then until the outbreak of the First World War, he ran in many stakes winning many Prizes and Certificates of Merit. Only one Trial was held during the War and that in aid of the Red Cross. Mr Kent won this event with an English Springer (Walhampton Croy) and during the Second World War when a similar Trial was run, he won again with a Springer (Teggie of Chrishall). Prior to World War I, Mr Kent could count amongst his competitors people such as Mr John Forbes, Mr R. Hill, Mr T. Gaunt, Mr J. Scott and Mr T. Ellis together with two I will mention later, Lorna, Countess Howe and Mr T. J. Greatorex. My memories of Mr Kent are of a very kind man to whom one went for advice as a novice and was never refused courtesy and practical help.

The First World War now made a break in the Trial careers of a number of dogs.

After the War and in the 1920s a number of prefixes became prominent. Lorna, Countess Howe, better known in later years for her Labradors, owned a number of Springers the best known being F.T. Ch. Banchory Bright. This bitch won the Spaniel Championship twice and a total of thirty three stakes. Her pedigree on both sides carried blood lines of Denne, Rivington and Avendale. Lady Howe was the Chairman of E.S.S.C.

Capt. O. P. Treherne owned the *Bryngarw* prefix and was for some years President of the English Springer Spaniel Club. Five of his dogs, F.T. Champions Bryngarw Coleraine, Bryngarw Jack, Bryngarw Firearm, Bryngarw Firefly and Bryngarw Firelight were all winning stakes in the mid-twenties.

The *Downton* prefix was owned by Sir W. Rouse Boughton who took the name from his home Downton Hall, near Ludlow in Shropshire. Members of the family are members of the English Springer Spaniel

F.T. Ch. Bryngarw
Firearm owned by
the late Capt. O. P.
Treherne.

Club to this day. He ran many dogs at Field Trials and also competed
at Shows during the 1920s when his Downton Darkie, Downtown
Duckets and a dog called Tinker were all well known. One of his
breeding, Downton Flash, was sold to Mr A. L. Trotter who changed
its name under Kennel Club Rules then in force and it became very
well known as F. T. Ch. Dalshangar Dandy Boy.

Mr A. L. Trotter, who bought Downton Flash from the Rouse Boughton Kennel was the owner of the *Dalshangar* prefix. Having obtained F.T. Championship status with Dandy Boy he sold him to the States where he sired a number of winners including a F.T. Champion.

The *Horsford* prefix owned by Mr William Humphrey needs special mention because it produced the second of the three Dual Champions in the breed, namely Dual Ch. Horsford Hetman. Apart from this, of course, William Humphrey was one of the breed's great characters and an expert falconer.

At this point, although a little out of order I would like to mention Lt. Colonel F. B. H. Carrell's *of Harting* suffix because of this line came our third and final Dual Champion—Dual Champion Thoughtful of Harting. Remember these three – Dual Champions Horsford Hetman, Thoughtful of Harting and Flint of Avendale, for I doubt that we shall see their like again.

Only a short time ago I was looking up some Field Trial pedigrees and there was mention of Mr David McDonald's prefix *L'ile*. All his dogs were workers and he also carried off a lot of awards on the bench. His Ch. Little Brand has already been mentioned elsewhere in this text.

Another prefix of note in the mid 1920s was Mr W. D. Edwards' *Pierpoint*. He seldom missed a trial and notched up many wins. F.T. Ch. Pierpoint Splint, Pierpoint Brand and Pierpoint Perfection were three well known winners.

Immediately prior to the Second World War two strains were prominent. First the *Tedwyns* prefix of Mr A. Bryne who was running F.T. Ch. Tedwyns Trex and other such as Tedwyns Trick and Tedwyns Togs. The second is that famous *O'Vara* prefix owned by Mr Selwyn C. Jones and right up to the Second World War the O'Vara strain was leading the way with dogs such as Slack O'Vara, Slip O'Vara, Style O'Vara, Trout O'Vara and so many more. The O'Vara dogs were always handled by that grand old gentleman, Mr. T. J. Greatorex, who was for many years Secretary of the Spaniel Club. His own *Corndean* prefix was also well known in Field Trial circles and when Mr Jones died in the late 1950s, the O'Vara prefix was passed to him. Only a brief glance at Field Trial pedigrees is needed to see the dominance of the O'Vara line.

I believe that the O'Vara kennel still holds the record number of Field Trial Champions in this country and the K.C. Spaniel Championship has been won seven times. One dog, F.T. Ch. Scramble O'Vara won it twice.

Mr John Forbes trained and handled for other people but had his own *Glennewton* prefix. For many years he was associated with Commander Collard's *Elan* stock and made up two Springer F.T. Champions—Rossend Prince and Richard of Elan.

Mr J. Kent's F.T. Ch. Silverstar of Chrishall.

Mr Reg Hill was training and handling dogs at Trials before the First World War and handled Triple F.T. Ch. Wake Wager to the top. I first made real contact with Mr Hill in the early part of the Second World War. He was at that time looking after the guard dogs at Rotol Airscrews on the Staverton Aerodrome near Cheltenham. I was then Secretary to Lt. Col. Baldwin, world famous for his Picardy Alsatians. The Colonel was then Commandant of the Ministry of Aircraft Production's Guard Dog Training School at Down Hatherley, so of course, the meetings with Mr Hill were not infrequent. Incidentally it was the Colonel who first set down for me the planning of a breeding programme. He was a most interesting man on the subject of pedigrees and the knowledge I gained from him was immense. Ever since then I have, of course, always had a soft spot for a good Alsatian.

In the years that followed the First World War the *Blair* prefix owned by Mr G. Clark was prominent. F.T. Ch. Bee of Blair won over a dozen Stakes and was the dam of F.T. Ch. Beeson of Blair who won the Spaniel Championship in 1935. They also figure in the pedigree of Mr John Kent's F.T. Ch. Silverstar of Chrishall. I mention this in particular as I would like to instance an attempt at this time to bring the show and working lines together again. Silverstar figures in many pedigrees today and not only in those of Field Trial dogs.

I have mentioned elsewhere that both Miss Francis and Miss Hooper were determined to try and combine the show and working qualities. Miss Francis mated her Ch. Higham Topsy to Silverstar and the

The late Miss C. M. Francis' Higham Tit Bit in action in the 1956 English Springer Club Trials.

mating produced Higham Tit Bit who won five Stakes and cards at shows. Another from the same litter was sold to Mr D. C. Hannah, was registered as Stokeley Higham Tonga, and eventually won second place in the Spaniel Championship. Miss Hooper mated her Reverie of Ranscombe to Silverstar and from the litter produced Runner of Ranscombe who won three Stakes, was third in another and reserve in two. He later went to the States.

Mr Lewis Wigan was running at Trials before 1914 and his successful dogs were running again after the War. Mr J. Scott Senr. handled an outstanding dog F.T. Ch. Jed of the Cairnies for Mr Wigan. This dog later sired Staindrop Spitfire whose name appears so frequently in Field Trial pedigrees.

In the late 1920s the *Wakefares* prefix owned by Mr F. M. Prime, made its appearance at Trials and began to build up a success story with a dog called Thrimley Joe. Under Kennel Club rules at that time it was necessary for a dog to win three Open Stakes to qualify for its title and this Joe did but unfortunately one of the Stakes was not fully subscribed and with only seven dogs running instead of eight, the qualification was not awarded. F.T. Ch. Wakes Wager qualified here and then went first to India and then to the States where he also qualified. He was, I believe, the only Springer to become a Triple Int. F.T. Champion. F.T. Ch. Wakefares Sprigg was another well known dog from this kennel. It was Mr Prime who gave me my first Qualifying Certificate with my Larkstoke Sugarcandy.

Between the two World Wars and afterwards a whole host of names appear in the winning records; Mr Andrew Wylie and his brother Jimmy, Mr A. E. Curtis, Mr Jack Chudley and his brother Keith, Mr J. Scott, Jnr., Mr T. B. Laird, Mr G. Curle, Mr W. D. Edwards, Mr W. G. Sheldon, Mr Hal Jackson, Major Hugh Peacock, Mr W. G. Fiske, Mr and Mrs R. B. Weston-Webb.

The Wylie brothers set up the *Pinehawk* kennels in the early 1930s and have produced a long line of Field Trial winners. The first dog to be made up after the Second World War was F.T. Ch. Pinehawk Roger. Many have followed including F.T. Ch. Acheson Trick, F.T. Ch. Ludlovian Socks, F.T. Ch. Pinehawk Sark and F.T. Ch. Pinehawk Spur.

The *Breckonhill* prefix was owned by Mr G. Curle and the kennel has produced several F.T. Champions including Breckonhill Bee, Breckonhill Brave, Breckonhill Bridegroom and Breckonhill Bilko.

F.T. Ch. Rivington Glensaugh Glean appears in so many pedigrees that he needs a special mention. He has sired at least eight Field Trial Champions and won the Spaniel Championship in 1951. He was owned by Messrs. E. & M. Ainsworth and bred by Mr D. Munro.

Mr Hal Jackson started in Field Trials in the early 1920s and his *Barnacre* suffix came into prominence when he won the Spaniel Championship in 1957 with F.T. Ch. Gwen of Barnacre and again in 1959 with her son F.T. Ch. Willy of Barnacre. A considerable record was achieved by Mr T. B. Laird after the Second World War. He owned, bred and trained seven Field Trial Champions which, of course, carried his *Criffel* prefix. These were F.T. Champions Criffel Daisy Bell, Pamela, Nellie, Prince, Danny, Snipe and Melody. Later he added Patsy, Ruth and Cherry.

The *Whittelmoor* dogs were owned by Mr A. E. Curtis who started his kennel in the late 1920s. He began training and handling for other owners and his first success came when he made Donna Susie into a F.T. Champion for her owner, Colonel McNeill. Later he made up two more of his own, F.T. Ch. Whittelmoor Record and F.T. Ch. Whittelmoor George. The latter was exported to the States where in 1950 he won the U.S.A. National Championship.

In the early 1960s a very nice looking Trial dog was making his name. It was F.T. Ch. Markdown Muffin owned by Mr F. Thomas, trained and handled by Mr John MacQueen, Junr. This dog, after being Second in the K.C. Championship Stake in 1961 won the event the following year. There are not many Trials that John MacQueen misses and he is a popular judge of Trials at the present time. Others carrying the prefix were F.T. Ch. Markdown Meg and F.T. Ch. Markdown Marcus. Major Hugh Peacock made up two F.T. Champions in the post-Second War period. One was F.T. Ch. Greatford Kim and the other F.T. Ch. Greatford Meadowcourt Stephen bred by Mr and Mrs R. B. Weston-Webb of whom more later. Major Peacock supported the English Springer for many years but he was better known for the F.T. Champions that he made up in Cockers and Labradors.

In the mid 1950s Mr Talbot Radcliffe brought his *Saighton* prefix into prominence by making a F.T. Champion of Saighton's Sentry. Since then others have been added including F.T. Champion Saighton's Scent, Saulson, Spree, Swing, and Stinger. I shall always be appreciative for the kindness Mr Radcliffe extended to me when he allowed me to go over to Angelsey and take my Larkstoke Willywicket with me to do some training and work on land and water. Mr Radcliffe has always spoken his mind on the subject of show and working strains

F.T. Ch. Saighton's Swing owned by Mr Talbot Radcliffe.

Dauntless Monty
owned by the late
Mr W. G. Sheldon.

and I felt it a compliment that he gave me his time and expressed some
positive comment on my dog's ability in the field.

Mr R. N. Burton from Lazonby in Cumbria had a successful run in
Trials. His prefix is *Brackenbank* and perhaps his best known winner
was F.T. Ch. Brackenbank Tangle for after being exported to the
States it won the U.S.A. Championship in 1957. Here it is interesting
to note that this classic American Stake has been won by a number of
exports from this country. As in the show world, some of our best
stock has gone across the water to form the foundation of successful
lines over there.

The *Meadowcourt* prefix of Mr and Mrs R. B. Weston-Webb was
well known in Cockers when they began to support the Springer Trials.
The kennel produced a number of winners including F.T. Ch.
Meadowcourt Judy, F.T. Ch. Meadowcourt Polly, F.T. Ch. Meadowcourt Della, F.T. Ch. Meadowcourt Wendy, and F.T. Ch. Blatherwycke Meadowcourt Hector owned by Mrs Frank George. Judy was
placed second in the K.C. Spaniel Championship in 1962.

At the end of the 1940s and into the 1950s the *Ludlovian* prefix of
Mr W. G. Sheldon was prominent. His first dog Ludlow Gyp was
trained by Mr Jimmy Wylie but after that everything that carried the
Ludlovian prefix was bred, trained and handled by Mr Sheldon
himself. His F.T. Champions were Dauntless Monty, Ludlow Gyp,

A fine group of Field Trial English Springers owned by the late Mr W. G. Sheldon.

Ludlovian Darkie, Ludlovian Ruby and Ludlovian Bruce. The latter was exported to the States and was another winner of the U.S.A. National Championship in 1954 and 1955. Within a short interval of time, five more Ludlovian exports were placed in the same event; F.T. Ch. Ludlovian Socks was placed third in 1956 and second in 1957 while F.T. Ch. Ludlovian Scamp was placed third in 1957. Mr Sheldon died in 1955 but had earned a great respect in the breed after only a short time of participation.

I have already mentioned Mrs Frank George as the owner of F.T. Ch. Blatherwycke Hector bred by Mrs R. B. Weston-Webb. Her husband, an extremely busy businessman connected with the management of Whitworth Foods, started his success in Trials with F.T. Ch. Streonshalh Comet and was placed with her at the K.C. Spaniel Championships in three successive years. His own prefix was *Wilby* and F.T. Ch. Wilby Trigger was bought as a youngster from Dr T. K. Davidson. His other winners included F.T. Ch. Harpersbrook Boots, F.T. Ch. Entonlee Cherry, F.T. Ch. Shineradee and F.T. Ch. Harpersbrook Reed. The latter won the K.C. Spaniel Championship in 1961. Mr George was extremely generous in his support of Trials and the English Springer Spaniel Club in particular was appreciative of the support he offered. I well remember the time when Mr George provided a large marquee and a marvellous range of refreshments for the Club's Trials when they were held on his shoot. Every Christmas there was a beautiful calendar from Mr George showing his Labradors and Springers. The calendar was prepared from prints taken from especially commissioned works and I was very taken with the one showing F.T. Ch. Harpersbrook Reed at work and I have since had it framed. It may not be generally known but Mr George was also a great fancier of racing pigeons and held a vast number of trophies confirming his success in that field. It is impossible, of course, to mention Mr and Mrs George without mention of the Chudley brothers, Jack and Keith. They set up their Harpersbrook kennels immediately after the Second World War and within the space of a few years were training and handling a number of successful Springers. They trained and handled all of Mr and Mrs George's dogs and it may be of interest to note that some dogs are still being run under the registered ownership of 'The Executors of the late F. George'. The Chudleys also trained and handled F.T. Ch. Greatford Kim for Major Peacock, F.T. Ch. Bryanston Bess for Mr D. Bowlby and F.T. Ch. Harpersbrook Sammy for Dr J. Hurndall Gann.

Whilst I was at the M.A.P. Guard Dog Training School with Lt. Colonel Baldwin, Mr Jack Chudley was at the War Dogs Training School where Mr H. S. Lloyd 'of Ware' was in charge of the training for the War Office. Whilst we at the Guard Dog Training School were training dogs for guard duties at factories and airfields, the War Dogs School was training for mine detection. Mr Chudley and I had many acquaintances in common and a number of well known present judges of trials and shows were associated with these two Schools. A former Secretary of the Kennel Club, Mr Ted Holland Buckley, was commissioned in the Army and worked with Mr H. S. Lloyd. Whilst at the Guard Dog Training School we at one time took on the staff a grandson of Charles Cruft who founded the great show that took his name.

In Chapter 3 I mentioned the Stokeley kennel of Mr D. C. Hannah as an example of the amalgamation of work and show and I would like to expand my comment in this chapter with particular emphasis on the working side. Ch. Stokeley Lucky won twenty-four awards at Field Trials and I have already mentioned the breeding programme that produced Stokeley Higham Tonga, later to be placed second in the 1958 K.C. Spaniel Championship. Tonga was dam to two Field Trials winners Rogue and Scamp later to be exported to Italy. In 1960 Stokeley Rogue won the International Field Trial near Milano and another Stokeley export Stokeley Speed was placed third. Yet another export, Stokeley Marco became an Italian Champion winning three

Messrs Hampton
and Harris' F.T.
winner Rossmelas of
Larkstoke.

open stakes and two challenge certificates. The owner of the Stokeleys
in Italy is Sig. Marco Valcarenghi who came to England and stayed
with Mr and Mrs Hannah on many occasions to gain knowledge of the
breed before taking stock back to Italy. Sig. Valcarenghi returns to
England at intervals when he has accepted invitations to judge the
breed at some of the Championship Shows.

Many years ago now I sold a puppy to Mrs Margaret (Peggy) Pratt
from Stourport and I have maintained a friendship with her and her
husband John ever since. The Pratts farmed in Worcestershire and
perhaps it was only natural that within a few years of keeping Springers
and entering for some of the Shows, that their interest turned to the
shooting dog and Trials. She bought Stokeley Sultan from Mr Hannah,
won some prizes at shows and entered him in an Amateur Handlers'
Stake. In the late 1950s she went to Miss Francis and bought Higham
Tally which she took home and trained herself. Two seasons later she
had won a number of awards at Trials and a Diploma at the K.C.
Spaniel Championship. Her next purchase was Posterngate Jo from Dr
Douglas White and success was steady, backed by a great enthusiasm.
Since that time Peggy and John have trained and handled stock
carrying the *Bricksclose* prefix leading to success with F.T. Ch.

Bricksclose Scilla, F.T. Ch. Bricksclose Scout and Bricksclose Midi-Too. A litter brother to Midi-Too is Bricksclose Mark and I have used this dog on some of my own stock. We now have two Field Triallers, a dog and bitch, sired by the Bricksclose line and held in partnership between my husband and Mr Martin Harris who takes on the training and handling and we have had a number of successes.

Mention of Mrs Pratt's purchase from Dr Douglas White brings an interesting point to mind. In the show world we seem to collect a high percentage of people who are connected with education, especially in the show management side, and for some reason or other it sems that the medics are drawn to the Field Trial side. In the last War and just after the Clubs counted Dr Goodwin and Dr Sunderland amongst their members. Then there were Dr Edmondson and Dr Hurndall Gann, already mentioned, as the owner of F.T. Ch. Harpersbrook Sammy. Dr T. K. Davidson has had many winners with his *Jonkit* prefix notably F.T. Ch. Jonkit Jasper, F.T. Ch. Jonkit Jandy (owned by Mr B. B. Dutton) and F.T. Ch. Jonkit Joel. Dr Douglas White, a great character at the trials, has produced many winners carrying his *Posterngate* prefix, notably F.T. Ch. Posterngate Jet. In more recent times Dr Diana Bovill has had a great deal of success with her F.T. Ch. Harwes Mitten, F.T. Ch. Harwes Silver and F.T. Ch. Harwes Silas. She has worked very closely with Mr Douglas Hurst who with

Bricksclose Masterpiece (left) and Bricksclose Mark.

his brother Alan are well known trainers and handlers of trial dogs. One of the latest medical arrivals is Dr Michael Budden.

Another great supporter of trials in the mid 1900s was Mrs P. M. Badenach Nicolson who made up F.T. Ch. Carswell Cornelia, F.T. Ch. Carswell Contessa and F.T. Ch. Carswell Blanche. The latter was yet another to be exported to the States and to win the U.S.A. National Championship.

Mr Bernard Dutton has bred a few trial winners. His best known was F.T. Ch. Hamers Hansel when he won the Spaniel Championship. Earlier I mentioned the record of Mr T. B. Laird with the seven Criffel F.T. Champions and later additions. This brings me to quite a remarkable dog called Hales Smut owned by Mr Arthur Cooke. Smut's pedigree goes back to the O'Vara line but he was bred by Mr Keith Erlandson who sold him as a pup to Mr Frank Bell. He changed hands again finishing with Arthur Cooke who trained and handled him at trials. This dog has now sired certainly thirteen Field Trial Champions. He ran for four seasons and won seventeen awards but he never won a stake. He must surely be one of the greatest influences in field trial dogs of recent years. Lt. Colonel Lewin Spittle, who succeeded Miss Hooper as Field Trial Secretary to the English Springer Spaniel Club, bred and owned F.T. Ch. Gwibernant Garren. He also owned F.T. Ch. Dinas Dewi Sele bred by Mr William Llewellyn. All his dogs were trained and handled by Mr Keith Erlandson of the *Gwibernant* prefix. Mr Erlandson bought Abereithy Skip from Mr Llewellyn, added his own prefix and made the dog up into a Field Trial Champion. He also bred F.T. Ch. Gwibernant Fynon (owned by Mr R. Fettis) and F.T. Ch. Lancshot Laser (owned by Mr C. C. Lamb). A well known winner and sire was Capt. Lansdale's F.T. Ch. Temple Grafton Hardy bred by Mrs W. H. Whitbread. Mr J. W. Davey produced a nice winning bitch in F.T. Ch. Wivenwood Fofo. Mrs C. A. Thomson from Scotland bred F.T. Ch. Rivington Raechele and F.T. Ch. Rivington Judy and Mr Frank Bell bred F.T. Ch. Shineradee for Mr F. George.

There follow a great many triallers who have gained the title with one or two dogs and maybe have never won the title but have been producing good sound working stock. It is difficult to include all and my apologies to those who may feel that they ought to have been included. I will conclude my detail of winning lines with a few of these that have been more prominent in recent years and others who are better known in the training field. First I would mention three of the great stud dogs Hales Smut; Mr J. Magree's F.T. Ch. Slingay of Ardoen bred by Mr W. Sloan and Mr Sloan's own F.T. Ch. Lady of Ardoen bred by Mrs Spittle and Capt. R. Corbett's F.T. Ch. Micklewood Story.

Mrs E. M. Hartt bred and owned F.T. Ch. Braiswood Mattie, she

F.T. Ch. Crowhill Raffles owned by Mr P. Stewart.

also bred F.T. Ch. Philray Tern (owned by Mr P. R. Elsey), F.T. Ch. Braiswood Rivet of Copford (owned by Mr R. King) and she owned F.T. Ch. Braiswood Pimm (bred by Mr J. W. Davey). Another very strong supporter among the ladies is Mrs Rachel Gosling. Mr M. Scales bred, trained and handled his own F.T. Ch. Layerbrook Michelle another sired by Hales Smut.

Mr Maurice Hopper, well known as a trainer and author of a work on training, bred Lytchmore Logan which Mr F. George later made into a Field Trial Champion. Mr D. M. Douglas made up F.T. Ch. Donhead Warrior and F.T. Ch. Donhead Walnut the latter being owned by Mr G. S. Drummond.

Mr W. Charles Williams has been a great supporter of trials for many years and most of his dogs have been trained and handled by Mr R. Male. From his combination came F.T. Ch. Temple Grafton Hardy, F.T. Ch. Berrystead Finch (bred by Mr J. W. Davey) and F.T. Ch. Berrystead Freckle (bred by Dr T. K. Davidson).

Messrs. J. and F. Orr between them produced F.T. Ch. Highland Boy and F.T. Ch. Sprig of Inler. The *Ballyrobert* prefix of Mr R. E. Clemitson has done its share of winning and he made up F.T. Ch. Ballyrobert Ben and F.T. Ch. Ballyrobert Chris. Mr R. Fairfax Naylor made up F.T. Ch. Rytex Rex bred by Mr D. Pemberton, trained and handled by Mr John MacQueen. F.T. Ch. Lewston Paul bred by Mr Stanley Lewis was made into a Field Trial Champion by his owner, Mr H. T. Hardwicke. Finally two more sired by Hales Smut are Mr T. B. Laird's F.T. Ch. Farway Skipper and F.T. Ch. Farway Shann.

Mr Richard Eversfield of the *Pinewarren* kennels has been active as a trainer and trialler for many years and he has been very helpful to the show people who want to do something about the working ability of their dogs.

When dealing with the Show Springer I went into some detail as to ring craft, etc. and so I thought it would be helpful to the lay reader if I quoted from an article I had previously written regarding the organisation of Field Trials in general and as they apply to English Springers.

The English Springer Spaniel is the dog most widely used of the Spaniel variety in Great Britain by the rough shooter, i.e. the man who goes out by himself or with a few friends in search of game, be it fur or feather, as opposed to the person who shoots at a more formal event when beaters are employed to drive the game over the standing guns, when dogs of the Retriever variety are more popular.

A Spaniel Trial is judged by two Judges with a Referee to adjudicate if the Judges cannot agree on the placings of the dogs. The Referee has no part in the placings of the dogs unless asked by the two Judges to make a decision. The dogs work in pairs, one under each Judge; the 'odd' numbers on the right and the 'even' numbers on the left. When a Judge has seen all the 'odd' or 'even' numbered dogs, he then takes the dogs which have been working under his colleague, so each dog works under both Judges during the Trial. However, if a dog has been eliminated for a disqualifying fault under one Judge the animal is not required to work under the other Judge.

The Spaniel must hunt his ground thoroughly, that is approximately 15 metres to either side of the handler, so that game which he flushes is within range when the shot can be taken. The dog must ignore lines and foot scent and leave no holding cover uninvestigated. If the dog misses game on his beat he will be marked down.

The dog must sit or drop when he flushes game, as well as to shot. Only on command should a dog go and retrieve game. To chase would mean elimination. To move more than a step or two towards flushed game is considered a major fault. A judge will, however, allow a dog to move to the edge of a bush from which he has flushed game, in order to view the fall. Pegging a bird or rabbit (i.e. catching it instead of flushing) is a disqualification. If a dog returns with game which has not been shot to him when in the process of hunting in the line, the Judge will examine the game and if he is satisfied that it is a wounded bird, the dog will be allowed to continue. A hard mouth is another fault which will disqualify. A judge will examine the game to see if it has crushed ribs etc., and will consult with his colleague on this point. A dog which 'gives tongue', whines, barks, etc., is also disqualified.

The Judges are looking for the dog which is under good control and works his ground with pace and style and will put game into the bag with the minimum delay.

If water is encountered during the Trial a dog will be expected to retrieve game from it. If he refuses he will be eliminated. One thing which a Judge would not ask a Competitor to do at a Spaniel Trial would be to send a dog for a long, 'blind' and 'not marked' retrieve. If a Judge has marked a fall a long distance away he would take the handler to within a reasonable retrieving distance before sending the dog.

When the Judges have seen all the dogs, they will compare their markings. It may be that they have a dog which has had a very good run under each of them and is considered to be the outright winner, in which case they will not require the dog to run again. Dogs of equal marks will be required to 'run-off' against each other but this time the dogs will work close together and the Judges will walk together and assess the merit of the dogs when the main considerations will be style, pace and ground treatment. In this way the placings will be determined.

A Spaniel attains the title of Field Trial Champion when he has won two Open or All Aged Stakes; a dog which wins the Spaniel Championship also gains his title. Before being awarded his title a dog must have passed a Water Test to prove that he will enter water freely and swim. A Water Test Certificate can be obtained in normal competition at a Field Trial or at a special test at which two "A" Judges officiate.

The number of dogs allowed to run in a Stake is limited to 16 each day. The time allowed under each Judge is approximately 15 minutes, depending on the quantity of game and conditions of the ground.

The end of the Trial Season culminates with the Spaniel Championship organised by the Kennel Club. This is not absolutely accurate as over the past few years the Spaniel Club has organised the event on behalf of the Kennel Club and all the Field Trial Societies and Clubs holding Trials have "donated" towards the costs. Mr T. J. Greatorex was Secretary to the Spaniel Club for many years but now Mr C. Sutcliffe has taken over. The Championship is run in two parts, first a stake for Cockers and then a stake for Any Variety Spaniel other than Cockers. The Field Trial Council of the Kennel Club nominates eight possible judges taken from the Spaniel Panel A. These judges are elected by ballot by the Committees of the various Spaniel Societies entitled to qualify dogs for the title of Field Trial Champion. The area for the event has to be fairly extensive and at the same time very similar in ground cover in order that all the dogs may have, as far as possible, the same testing. The ground I like best for the event is at Blenheim Park, Woodstock and Shadwell, Thetford. Ground cover is similar, the area is vast and spectators get a chance to see what is going on. As the Championship is held in January at the end of the shooting season the weather can be anyone's guess. I have attended on bright, sunny and crisp snowy mornings, or when it has been biting cold with very heavy frost and then there are times when you are in for a soaking. The Any Variety Open Stake and the Cocker Stake alternate in being the first on the card each year. The Secretary and other officials will have the draw to establish individual order of running for each dog some days before printing the card which is the equivalent of the Show catalogue. Then the Trial is under way and operating as I have already described. When the judging is complete and the Judges have made a final decision the Secretary of the meeting will be called and given the results. There will be the usual First, Second, Third and Reserve awards plus Diplomas of Merit. The latter are only given at the Spaniel Championship. When all is done there is much to discuss. No matter whether it be a show, a trial or a game of bridge, there is always a looking back and a discussion. It is part of the game and I hope a valuable part. However, as was said about the shows, the judge in the ring is the only person to handle the dog and at a trial the judges are the people who see everything that the dog does throughout the day and they will decide on the best all-round performance.

One wonders sometimes about the future of trials. I am sure that they are a very important part of the work of any Spaniel Society, but as the years go on the availability of suitable ground becomes less. For so many years we have relied on the generosity of a somewhat small group of gentlemen with large estates and groups of gentlemen with shooting syndicates to allow us to use their land and shoot their game that has cost hard cash to put into the air. As the interest in working dogs and trials continues to grow I doubt whether availability of ground can keep pace with demand. For the Clubs and Societies, even without the cost of the ground, the charge upon the general funds is becoming excessive. It has heartened me as a former Breed Club Secretary to know that triallers realise the problems and have always been willing to increase their entry fees to help meet the problem. The show people have never, in my experience, been quite so willing to accept the situation. The Field Trial Secretary of any Club or Society must give a great deal of time to a trial before, during and after the event and may well be away from home for three days. It is not so easy to find people willing to accept such a commitment these days and we should pay tribute to those who do. As far as our Springers are concerned I would like to mention Mr F. J. (Joe) Robinson who acts as Field Trial Secretary to the English Springer Spaniel Club. He started with a show dog Chipmunk of Stubham and made him into a Champion. As a shooting man, Joe's dog had to work and he trained Chipmunk and took him along to the Spaniel Field Day where he won the Advanced Stake and Best Performance of the Day. From then on he gradually eased into the trial world and bought in field trial blood lines. When Colonel Spittle could not continue in office Joe took over. I think it was two seasons ago now when he won his first Novice Stake. A similar commitment was accepted by Mrs Jean Oakey who for many years now has been Field Trial Secretary to the Midland English Springer Spaniel Society.

In May 1978 Mr Wilson Stephens, former editor of *The Field*, took some figures from the 1976 edition, and then the latest, of the Kennel Club Stud Book. I would like to quote the following from his article:

> In the Gundog Group these breeds which have lost their working potential tend to become the smallest. In such numerically small breeds as Curly Coated Retrievers, Clumber and Sussex Spaniels, the working capacity is peripheral, if not extinct. Where the working capacity is the strongest the breeds are also the largest.

Mr Stephens then goes on to quote figures for Labradors to illustrate his point and then comes back to the particular:

> In Spaniels 315 English Springers gained entry (to the Stud book) — 98 show dogs (43 dogs and 55 bitches) against 217 field triallers (100 dogs and 117 bitches) giving a ratio of more than 2 to 1 in favour of the field triallers. The show English Springer and the working English Springer are virtually distinct breeds — to say which is to state the self-evident and is no disparagement of either. However, it explains why occasional plaintiveness from the show

side that the working type are 'not in accordance with the breed standard' fall on deaf ears. Field Trial English Springers are only the tip of an iceberg of an immensely larger population of pedigree working English Springers in action with the gun which do not run in trials, whereas there is no alternative to the ring as a *raison d'etre* for more than a few of the show variety.

I am sure that Mr Stephens has a very strong argument here and a rough check of the editions would appear to support this theory. We are well aware that under the old system for the Allocation of Challenge Certificates in the show world we would never have had so many had it not been for the number of field trial dog registrations. It is, of course, quite true that the English Springer occupies a place second to none in the shooting world as far as Spaniels are concerned. Whilst acknowledging the difference in type between show and working dogs I would still maintain that the difference need not be so marked as it is at the present time. I would maintain equally strongly that we must retain the working qualities even at the expense of some of the looks.

When I retired as Secretary of the English Springer Spaniel Club in July of 1978, Mr Wilson Stephens paid me a very nice compliment in a short paragraph in *The Field*. He was kind enough to say that I had retained the respect of both show and field trial enthusiasts throughout my term of office. He wondered how much more difficult that task had been because of the division in type. It was that much more difficult, of course, but I saw my over-riding task as that of maintaining the unity of the breed for I saw a possible break and split as a catastrophe for the breed as a whole and one which, in the long run, would bring the greatest harm to the Springer that was kept solely for show.

5 Choosing a Puppy

First of all I would ask the prospective buyer of a Springer puppy to be sure that they will be able to give the adult dog the type of life it ought to have. If you live in a flat or in the centre of a large city I would not recommend a Springer. Of course the breed will adapt to almost any environment but as a working dog it needs access to open areas where it can have proper exercise and use its natural instincts for hunting and enjoying the natural scents of the countryside. No matter how well you treat your Springer you will never recompense him for the loss of his instinctive pleasures. Town parks and recreation fields are not a substitute for the real thing. Secondly, I would like the prospective buyer to be reasonably clear as to why they need a Springer. Do they need a pet, a show dog or have they an interest in Field Trials? How often it happens that a breeder sells a puppy as a pet only to discover at a later date that the new owner is taking it around the Shows and becoming disappointed at their lack of success. In Springers it would be essential to look for particular blood lines if you wanted to develop an interest in Field Trials.

Always it is worth repeating that it is better not to buy your puppy from a dog ranch or pet shop; go to a reputable breeder. If you have problems in finding addresses write to the Kennel Club and ask for your letter to be forwarded to the Secretary of the Breed Club. The Secretary will then put you in touch with a reliable breeder in your own area.

When you are looking at the puppies ask to see the dam and, if possible, the sire. If you want your puppy for show or as a future brood bitch, take advice from the breeder and buy the best that you can afford. However, do not be tempted by the most promising puppy if it appears to be nervous. The behaviour of a really nervous puppy is quite different from that of one which has had very little contact with the outside world. If you observe for a while, the latter will soon come to you and wag its tail. If it will not do this do not buy it.

A ten week old puppy should have a fairly long head with well defined stop. The fluting between the eyes should extend over the brow into the skull. Look for a good reach of neck, good ribs and good quarters that are well let down to the hocks. The shoulders should be well laid and sloping. The front legs should be straight but at this age the puppy will appear to have knobbly knees. When the dog is fully grown these 'knees' will have flattened into the leg. Look for nice rounded cat-like feet. Movement up to five months of age will be loose but it should be sound. The set of the tail is important and this should be a little below the level of the back and should be carried straight with a lively action. A tail that is set above the level of the back will be carried high and this is most objectionable in an adult dog. There also seems to be a tendency towards an aggressive nature in a dog with this tail carriage and there is nothing more difficult at a show than a dog that is always trying to pick a quarrel with its neighbour. When I am judging I will not tolerate this in the ring as it is quite contrary to what the nature of a gundog should be. Imagine taking a dog like that out for a day's shooting. It is quite impossible so look for even the 'mini' signs of aggressiveness amongst the puppies from which you are choosing your own.

Look for a nice tight eye, a loose sloppy eye rim is most objectionable as the dog gets older and in a working dog it offers less protection to the eye itself when the dog is working in brambles and thick cover. Take care to look for damp patches around the eyes as this may be an indication of entropian which is an in-turning of the eyelids.

A good shiny coat is an indication of good condition. A poor coat may be hiding a lot of scale and perhaps a few lice. Some bitches are carriers of lice and some of these will obviously transfer to puppies. They can be treated quite easily but a reputable breeder will have already done something about this. Avoid the pot-bellied puppy as it probably carries a lot of worms. All puppies need to be wormed but once again this should have been done by the breeder. Puppies should not have fleas and you would not be expecting to buy these as well. Avoid the puppy that appears to be snuffly or in anyway off colour, it is so easy to bring disease to any other dogs that you may have.

Any land Spaniel coat colour is acceptable except red and white which is the colour of the Welsh Springer. The most usual colour is liver and white but the popularity of the black and white has increased considerably over recent years and it is a coat which is somewhat easier to keep in good condition especially during the summer, when the liver coat tends to bleach in the sun. Liver white and tan and black, white and tan are very attractive markings. Always, of course, try to choose a puppy that is evenly marked.

There is always the decision as to the sex of the puppy you are buying. Quite often a great deal of fuss is made of the trouble that a bitch will be during those two occasions each year when she is in season. Generally speaking they are less trouble than dogs, equally intelligent and quite as faithful. A dog can be just as much a problem all the year round when bitches in the neighbourhood are coming into season at irregular intervals. For many years we did not keep a dog in the kennels and never kept a dog puppy. Then after an unfortunate whelping, during which we lost the dam, we were left with a single dog puppy which we hand reared and, although he was not outstanding in any way, he lived in the house until his death and developed a particular attachment to my husband. Since then we have kept another dog, but not in the house. This one has always lived in the kennel but became very much my dog. I mention these two examples where Springers of the male sex have formed very strong attachments to us but except for special circumstances we would retain our preference for the bitches.

Once you have chosen your puppy and taken him home arrange for his course of injections against hard-pad, hepatitis and leptospirosis to be commenced or completed as the case may be. The breeder will tell you what has been done already and advise you as to a veterinary surgeon who will see that things are done properly. Try to keep your puppy at home and out of contact with other dogs until he has had his injections and built up some of his own immunity to the common diseases. I have seen so many poor little puppies being carried or walked around agricultural shows by doting owners completely oblivious to the risks to which they expose their pet. I have even seen this at some shows and where else better to pick up infection? Perhaps I should say here that it is contrary to Kennel Club Show Regulations for any puppy under six months of age to be exhibited and no dog should be allowed inside a show unless it has been entered for that show. It does happen!

In Chapter 6 I will be making some comments on breeding but now that you have a puppy remember that a good one can easily be ruined by poor rearing. I have always maintained that an individual puppy can be reared like a baby. It needs proper feeding and proper regular attention. In its formative years, a child gains so much from its contact with adults and others of its own age. In much the same way a puppy needs play and rest and the contacts necessary to develop its intelligence. This, of course, is condensed into a much shorter period of time. I am always a little worried about a puppy going as a pet into a home where there are very young children. Unless the parents are quite strict about the puppy's routine it gets far too much play and very little rest. The Springer is extremely easy to house train and will make an excellent companion.

6 Breeding and Kennel Management

Before you decide to breed a litter erect your run and kennel. Puppies are endearing in the nest but mischievous and sometimes destructive. By the age of four or five weeks they will manage to climb over most obstacles. If they are used to being confined to a run at an early age they will never attempt to escape or even be noisy to come out.

The most effective unit I have constructed from past experience is as follows:

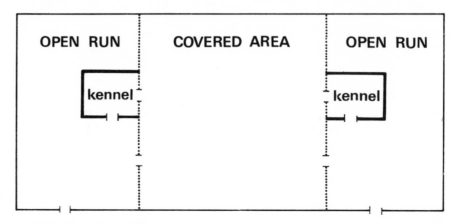

Fig. 8   Breeding Unit

When a litter is whelped the covered area can be halved by portable fencing and made into two complete units.

Accommodation for the stud dog should ideally be situated well away from the breeding unit.

Choice of Bitch

The bitch will come into season at any time from six months of age but should not be bred from until eighteen months to two years of age, and not after four years, for a first litter.

Take particular care in choosing your brood bitch. Find the type that you consider is nearest to the Standard, whether for work or show. See as many of the grandparents, great grandparents etc. as possible. These should be of the same type and, if possible, line bred, particularly the female side.

Check very carefully from breeders who have been associated with the breed for a long time and try to find out all you can about the family history of the blood lines in which you are interested. Make a very special effort to find out where the hereditary faults occur and pay particular attention to the following points:

a Temperament. No animal, however beautiful or clever, is of any pleasure to its owner if it is shy or snappy and unsafe with children and other livestock.
b Entropion. This is too often concealed by surgery. Untreated it is unsightly and most important of all, it causes pain to the animal. If you find this condition, do not accept any of the reasons or excuses that may be offered to you. This is an hereditary condition and must be avoided.
c Hip Dysplasia. Responsible breeders will have their stock X-rayed and most breed clubs will be able to supply a list of such breeders. It is well worth the extra time and effort involved in obtaining this additional information.
d Progressive Retinal Atrophy. Generally known by the initials P.R.A. this condition is blindness and can occur in stock from a few weeks in age. It is generally found in slightly older stock so check whether the stock you are looking over have P.R.A. Certificates, either Interim (3 years) or Permanent (5 years).

There is an old axiom that if one looks for an animal with a head like a lady's, a backside like a cook's, with a low set and low carried tail, one could not go far wrong. Mr William Arkwright summed up the latter beautifully when he said that is where the blue blood shows.

In addition to the points I have mentioned, the bitch should be well bodied, have good shoulders and above all good feet. After all, the latter have to carry all the rest of the body.

Choice of Stud Dog

The stud dog can usually be used from ten months for his first bitch. He should then have his second bitch not before another six months. After then, not more than twice a week.

Your stud dog should be chosen with as great care and time as the brood bitch. Check the pedigree for the same good points and faults that you were looking for in the bitch. There is an easy way to find the dominant blood lines using the following example pedigree overleaf:

Points Awarded

5	4	3	2	1
Arthur	Chris	{ Fred *Gwen*	etc.	etc.
	Donna	{ Harry *Gwen*		
Betty	Edward	{ Ivor Jane		
	Donna	{ Ken *Gwen*		

Award points to the pedigree starting with the parents of the proposed mating. Thus Donna would be awarded 8 points and Gwen 9 points. Both would have considerable influence on the resulting progeny.

You must always remember that you can always double the faults as well as the virtues.

The Mating

A young dog may be shy of his first two or three matings. If so absolute quiet is essential and some youngsters are better mated in the dark. After the tie the dog should be turned gently and the bitch prevented from sitting down. After mating the dog should be quietly walked about and returned to his kennel and the bitch should be rested.

Time of mating differs greatly from bitch to bitch. Usual time is twelve to fourteen days but some bitches will stand at eight or eighteen days. An expert will often be able to tell whether or not a litter is expected at three to three-and-a-half weeks. Most bitches do not show in whelp until six-and-a-half to seven weeks and after this time exercise should be resitricted.

Whelping

The following gestation and whelping time-table is a useful guide as to when puppies may be expected.

WHELPING TABLE

Jan. Served	March Due Whelp	Feb. Served	April Due Whelp	March Served	May Due Whelp	April Served	June Due Whelp	May Served	July Due Whelp	June Served	Aug. Due Whelp	July Served	Sept. Due Whelp	Aug. Served	Oct. Due Whelp	Sept. Served	Nov. Due Whelp	Oct. Served	Dec. Due Whelp	Nov. Served	Jan. Due Whelp	Dec. Served	Feb. Due Whelp
1	5	1	5	1	3	1	3	1	3	1	3	1	3	1	2	1	3	1	3	1	3	1	2
2	6	2	6	2	4	2	4	2	4	2	4	2	4	2	3	2	4	2	4	2	4	2	3
3	7	3	7	3	5	3	5	3	5	3	5	3	5	3	4	3	5	3	5	3	5	3	4
4	8	4	8	4	6	4	6	4	6	4	6	4	6	4	5	4	6	4	6	4	6	4	5
5	9	5	9	5	7	5	7	5	7	5	7	5	7	5	6	5	7	5	7	5	7	5	6
6	10	6	10	6	8	6	8	6	8	6	8	6	8	6	7	6	8	6	8	6	8	6	7
7	11	7	11	7	9	7	9	7	9	7	9	7	9	7	8	7	9	7	9	7	9	7	8
8	12	8	12	8	10	8	10	8	10	8	10	8	10	8	9	8	10	8	10	8	10	8	9
9	13	9	13	9	11	9	11	9	11	9	11	9	11	9	10	9	11	9	11	9	11	9	10
10	14	10	14	10	12	10	12	10	12	10	12	10	12	10	11	10	12	10	12	10	12	10	11
11	15	11	15	11	13	11	13	11	13	11	13	11	13	11	12	11	13	11	13	11	13	11	12
12	16	12	16	12	14	12	14	12	14	12	14	12	14	12	13	12	14	12	14	12	14	12	13
13	17	13	17	13	15	13	15	13	15	13	15	13	15	13	14	13	15	13	15	13	15	13	14
14	18	14	18	14	16	14	16	14	16	14	16	14	16	14	15	14	16	14	16	14	16	14	15
15	19	15	19	15	17	15	17	15	17	15	17	15	17	15	16	15	17	15	17	15	17	15	16
16	20	16	20	16	18	16	18	16	18	16	18	16	18	16	17	16	18	16	18	16	18	16	17
17	21	17	21	17	19	17	19	17	19	17	19	17	19	17	18	17	19	17	19	17	19	17	18
18	22	18	22	18	20	18	20	18	20	18	20	18	20	18	19	18	20	18	20	18	20	18	19
19	23	19	23	19	21	19	21	19	21	19	21	19	21	19	20	19	21	19	21	19	21	19	20
20	24	20	24	20	22	20	22	20	22	20	22	20	22	20	21	20	22	20	22	20	22	20	21
21	25	21	25	21	23	21	23	21	23	21	23	21	23	21	22	21	23	21	23	21	23	21	22
22	26	22	26	22	24	22	24	22	24	22	24	22	24	22	23	22	24	22	24	22	24	22	23
23	27	23	27	23	25	23	25	23	25	23	25	23	25	23	24	23	25	23	25	23	25	23	24
24	28	24	28	24	26	24	26	24	26	24	26	24	26	24	25	24	26	24	26	24	26	24	25
25	29	25	29	25	27	25	27	25	27	25	27	25	27	25	26	25	27	25	27	25	27	25	26
26	30	26	30	26	28	26	28	26	28	26	28	26	28	26	27	26	28	26	28	26	28	26	27
27	31	27	1 (May)	27	29	27	29	27	29	27	29	27	29	27	28	27	29	27	29	27	29	27	28
28	1 (April)	28	2	28	30	28	30	28	30	28	30	28	30	28	29	28	30	28	30	28	30	28	1 (March)
29	2			29	31	29	1 (July)	29	31	29	31	29	1 (Oct)	29	30	29	1 (Dec)	29	31	29	31	29	2
30	3			30	1 (June)	30	2	30	1 (Aug)	30	1 (Sept)	30	2	30	31	30	2	30	1 (Jan)	30	1 (Feb)	30	3
31	4			31	2			31	2			31	3	31	1 (Nov)			31	2			31	4

Some hours before whelping some bitches will be restless and try to make a bed. Some will not. When there is a sticky, starchy discharge the bitch should be removed to her whelping box in a quiet place. Stay with her until the first pup is born and make sure that she produces and eats the afterbirth.

Puppies should arrive at regular intervals. If there is more than two hours between puppies assistance should be sought.

When two or three puppies have been whelped it is advisable (if the bitch is not upset by your actions) to remove the older puppies and put them on a hot water bottle in a basket and cover with a cloth. They will soon settle down to sleep and will stay dry and warm until the last one is born. Then take the bitch out for a short walk and allow her to relieve herself. Return bitch and pups to a clean bed in a quiet and fairly dark place and allow them all to settle down.

For a first litter six or seven puppies is quite enough and it is wise to destroy any in excess of this number. Do not handle more than is necessary for the first week and make sure that the bitch remains quiet, warm and well nourished but not crammed with food. Keep the bitch clean and well groomed at all times and in fact I always make a point of washing the teats and clearing away any excessive underneath feathering a few days before whelping is expected to take place. I think it is very important that bitch and puppies should be in such a place as makes it possible for the bitch to relieve herself when and as often as necessary. A 'clean' bitch will become distressed if unable to do this without fouling the immediate vicinity of the kennel.

Do not expect all bitches to appear to have a lot of milk. Healthy puppies will take all the milk the bitch produces. If the pups are doing well they must be getting enough food.

Regulating the bitch's diet is of course important but generally there is no need to prepare special meals. It is advisable, however, when the end of pregnancy is in sight to divide the usual amount of food into two or three separate meals instead of the usual large one.

After whelping the bitch should be allowed to eat the after-birth and for the next twenty-four hours give light food such as milk and eggs and then gradually get back to the normal diet. Bitches will produce milk if fed on a well balanced proprietary food containing maize flake and meat. It is very important that there should always be an ample supply of fresh clean water.

If the puppies are sqeaking and appear to be hungry they should be examined for any abnormalities such as cleft palate etc. Any puppies like this should be destroyed. After two to three days the milk supply should have settled down and the bitch will want to leave her pups after feeding. She should be free to leave or stay at will. For the first week do not allow them to be handled nor shown off to strangers. Tails and dew claws should be removed at four days.

The correct length to dock is to remove 3/5ths. Blunt scissors should be used and permanganate of potash crystals rubbed into the cut. If this is done quickly there will be no bleeding and the bitch will not lick the puppies and stimulate any tendency to bleed. The puppies should be removed two or three at a time and returned to the bitch immediately. In this way she will not be caused any distress.

There is, of course, a great deal of controversy regarding the docking of tails and it must be said that we do not dock the tails on our English Springers for any aesthetic reason. The few Springers that I have seen that have not been docked looked very attractive and there is certainly nothing in the Standard to suggest that an undocked dog should be penalised in the show ring.

The reason for docking is to avoid damage to the tail when the dog is working in brambles and thick cover. The natural action of the tail is to beat to and fro and so it is very easy for a tail to become badly lacerated and this will be very painful for the dog.

A similar reason applies to the removal of the dew claws which should be done at the same time as docking. If a dew claw is left on the foot it can easily be torn while the dog is at work and even the house dog will find ways and means of causing damage to this part of the foot.

I often wish that some of the 'anti-dockers' would pause to give a little time and consideration to the reasons why we do certain things to our working dogs after which they might realise that we have the dogs' welfare at heart.

Feeding and Kennel Accommodation

If the puppies are contented and doing well it will not be necessary to feed them until four weeks of age. They can be started on a teaspoonful of raw meat twice a day whilst still being fed by the dam. Also give a small drink of any puppy milk or Nestlés Condensed mixed with warm water. By the end of the 4th or 5th week they should have two meals of Farex and milk plus two feeds of meat or meat, biscuit and gravy. At three months reduce to three feeds if they are well grown. Two feeds at six months and one at eighteen months.

Puppies should be wormed at three weeks and again at six weeks of age, and if necessary at ten weeks.

Puppies' claws should be kept short or the bitch will be scratched and will not settle to feed the puppies. She should be allowed to feed them as long as she will.

Do not show the bitch or let her run the risk of picking up any infection until the puppies are completely weaned. She can then be returned to the show ring but kept away from the puppies on her return.

Pups should be inoculated at twelve weeks and until then they should not be taken out. This poses problems in as much as some pups will appear to be nervous of the outside world.

If possible they should be taken out in the car so that they become used to it and the noises of the outside world. If you live in an isolated place arrange for them to go to training classes. Not so much for training but just to mix with other dogs. They will soon gain confidence. Ring training can be started at 5 to 6 months. Gundog training, provided that the pup has learnt to come when called, can start at 8 to 10 months.

The kennel accommodation I have described earlier in this Chapter is very suitable for the small breeder (or for a breeding unit) but if a number of dogs are going to be kept then a different and more extensive arrangement would be necessary. These days there is an extensive range of kennelling available from commercial sources which is well made and easily erected.

It is an advantage to site any range of kennels facing south and if possible to give shelter from the east and north winds in the winter. It follows that shading in the natural form of trees, or by some artificial means, is necessary during the summer months. In all events try to avoid siting which will exaggerate the seasonal conditions. If you are proposing to build a range of kennels from building blocks or brick then obviously you will need proper foundation footings, but even if you are erecting a portable wooden kennel I would recommend that it be stood on a concrete base. The run should be of concrete which has not been too smoothly surfaced so that it is not slippery in the wet. A slight slope away from the actual kennel will ensure proper drainage of any surface water after it has been raining. Earth runs are not suitable as they cannot be washed down and so create unhygenic conditions and in winter they will obviously be just a muddy patch. Concrete runs also help to keep a dog's claws short and the foot tight. If your Springer is one of those that likes to dig holes another obvious advantage comes to mind!

I always like to put down a small wooden platform for the dogs to lie on in a concrete run. A heavy dog throwing itself down on a hard surface will often develop hard bare patches on the elbows and rump.

It is a great advantage to have part of the run under cover so that the dogs can be outside in the fresh air even on a wet day.

ELEVATION

The kennel should have a large window in the front and this could commence some 3½ feet from ground level. There is some advantage in using iron bars for this window provided well fitting shutters are available for the winter months. The kennel door is better made in two halves, like a stable door, so that the top may be opened whilst the bottom is still closed. Inside the upper half door it is useful to have another half section set in iron bars so that the kennel may be closed and secured but the dogs have maximum light and air. It is useful to have a trap door in the bottom half of the door which is operated from

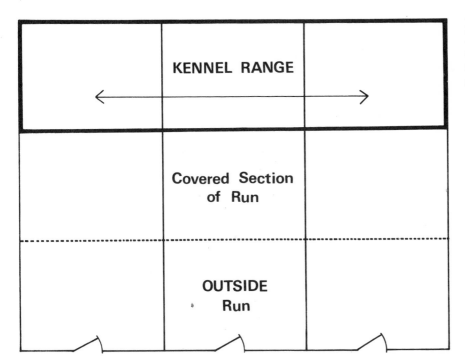

Fig. 9   Kennel Range. Kennel 6' x 6' square, 6' at front sloping to 5' 6'' at rear

the outside. This will allow the kennel to be aired without the main door being open. This is a most useful arrangement for a bitch with a litter of puppies who can run in and out at will and find protection from wind when inside the kennel. Remember that puppies will have difficulty in getting in an out unless a ramp is fixed from the base of the trap door to the level of the run outside. An important point to mention is the quality of the kennel construction. It must be well made and absolutely draught proof.

Bedding can be contained in one part of the kennel floor area by slipping a board between battens nailed to the side of the kennel.

For a bitch with puppies it is useful to cover the bed section with a boarded roof which is just laid on another set of battens nailed to the wall of the kennel. This gives the puppies protection from down draughts and quite often the bitch will like to jump up on the 'roof' to take a rest from her brood.

For many years I have used newspaper as bedding for puppies. When soiled it can be rolled up and burnt or disposed of in other ways. Some of the print may dirty the white parts of the puppies' coats but this soon wears off when the puppies are older and placed on other forms of bedding. I found other forms of bedding a little dusty and this tended to irritate the puppies' eyes. The latest product called Drybed appears to be very suitable and can easily be washed and kept clean.

For the adult dogs I do not think that there is better bedding than good clean long-stemmed oat straw. This keeps the coats in beautiful bloom and is, of course, ideal for the dogs after a day out in the wet with the gun. Never use barley or rye straw as this will work its way into the ears and cause other problems. Wood wool is suitable for adult dogs but not for puppies.

All wooden floors need to be kept clean and this must be done by scrubbing with hot water using soda or some form of disinfectant. In summer the wood dries quickly but in winter this is not so easy and puppies should not be put back into a damp bedding area. Dry sawdust can be used to mop up and then this is collected up and thrown away. The kennel floor can be covered liberally with sawdust before the dog returns. Good straw and good clean sawdust are not as easy to obtain as they used to be but it is well worth while looking around for a reliable and regular source.

All gates to kennel runs should open inwards so that if necessary a dog can be pushed back and you can step in sideways. This is really a safety precaution which a friend of mine has extended into a lock-gate system. That is to say she has two gates so that the first gate is shut before the second one is opened. This is particularly useful if you have dogs in the dog kennel that are not your own. If you do ever have to take your dog to a boarding kennel, keep your eye open as to what safety arrangements they employ. It is easy for a dog in strange surroundings to slip away when being exercised or moved to another kennel.

Your pet Springer, provided you have house trained him, can well live indoors without any special kennel accommodation. A bed that is slightly raised from the floor and placed in a quiet corner is very suitable. I prefer one of the folding iron framed beds with a stretched canvas side and base. The base can be covered with a blanket and this is easily removed for washing at regular intervals. From time to time the canvas base can be scrubbed and everything is as hygenic as possible. Dog baskets do collect dust and dirt and for this reason I prefer the canvas on a metal frame.

The latest idea of 'dog nests' are both hygienic and comfortable. They are also very good for transport to shows and ideal for dogs returning from a shoot. They are made of polystyrene beads in a canvas cover and will push into any shape.

A word about house training. This cannot be done without some effort on your part. Watch for the signs that the puppy needs to go out and let him out as often as possible. You will soon get into the routine and so will he. Always take your puppy outside immediately it wakes up from sleep and also after feeding. Stay with it until it has done what you require when you should praise it. If he does offend he must be scolded but nothing more severe is necessary. Give the scolding immediately after the offence and as near to it as possible. I said elsewhere that if you reared your puppy as you would a child you could not go far wrong.

I always feel that house training should have a slightly wider implication and I would extend it into general good behaviour. Personally I dislike going to somebody else's home to be greeted by a dog which jumps up at me and leaves dirty foot marks down a clean dress or pair of slacks. Our dogs can greet us without this rather annoying habit. I also object to moving the house dog off the armchair before I can sit down only to find myself covered in dog hairs when I leave. Meantime a perfectly clean and adequate dog's bed is vacant in the corner of the room. It is really only a matter of getting your dog used to a routine which in the long run makes life so much easier for everyone.

On the whole I expect that most Springers kept in the house are really overfed. As a breed they are not fussy eaters and there is little that they will refuse. As soon as my own dogs have reached adult stage they are fed only once a day. Just when feeding takes place is a matter of personal convenience and I have always fed about 4.00 p.m. in the winter and 5.00 p.m. in the summer months. The main thing is to keep to a regular pattern. For many years I fed raw horse meat giving about 1½ lb to each adult. When this became difficult to obtain I changed to tripe which was usually fed raw but quite often had to be cooked in the summer months. They made very good feed and the dogs liked them but they do smell and you really need separate cooking arrangements away from the house. Then tripe became difficult to obtain and I changed to one of the proprietary balanced meals which is scalded with boiling water and allowed to cool before use. Too much water makes the meal sloppy and unpalatable but fed at the right consistency is a good feed and all my dogs have maintained excellent condition. I believe in adding some vegetable matter such as cabbage, sprouts etc., from time to time and also a few drops of good quality cod liver oil. Some yeast in the form of tablets as marketed under one well known brand is another good additive at fairly regular intervals. A good supply of fresh clean water is essential. If the weather is very severe in winter the dogs have a warm drink late at night and early in the morning. This is prepared either from a proprietary brand containing mineral salts or milk powder.

Nothing is given between the once a day feeds unless I know that I may be late home from a show or otherwise away, in which case I will give a small feed of meal before I leave in the morning.

7 Common Ailments and Hereditary Faults

It may be as well to commence this chapter with the common ailments with which your Springer may come in contact and to deal with some hereditary faults later. In many ways the latter are far more important because these faults are only spread through the breeding programmes of individual breeders. A good working knowledge of the breed is desirable before embarking upon any breeding programme and this will help you to avoid certain bloodlines for particular reasons. You will, of course, wish to select certain blood lines for their good and positive characteristics.

A little knowledge is always helpful but as soon as you feel that the problem has developed beyond the simple stage always call in your veterinary surgeon. You may be causing unnecessary suffering to your dog, increasing the possibility of a long or fatal illness or of spreading disease to other dogs in the kennel. It is easy to notice when a dog is off colour and the first thing to do is to check the temperature so always have a half-minute clinical thermometer available. A dog's temperature is taken in the rectum and should be 101.4°F. If it should rise much above 103°F or fall below 100°F. you have cause for concern. Of course, a rise or fall in temperature must be related to other symptoms but generally these are warning signs.

Some fifty years ago much research was carried out on the distemper virus and we owe much to the veterinary scientists who found and perfected the distemper vaccine. It was a most unpleasant disease and I well remember the hours of care and attention given to suffering dogs. There were so many complications and a more virulent attack could often leave paralysis, enteritis, pneumonia or pleurisy. Later a very similar virus known as hard-pad appeared in kennels up and down the country and this also proved a killer disease. As the name implies, the pads hardened off and as a dog moved across a hard floor a peculiar tapping sound could be heard. I once nursed four young dogs through an attack of hard-pad but all were left with some problem and the mental strain was intense.

Much of the research work into canine medicine etc. is carried out by voluntary bodies and one cannot speak too highly of the Animal Health

Trust and its staff. Most breed clubs, throughout the country, support the Trust with annual donations and certainly the English Springer Spaniel Club has done so for many years.

Some diseases are infectious and contagious and the most common are:-

Hepatitis. This virus, common to all dogs, induces a fever giving temperature rises up to 104°F. Usually the liver is attacked and the dog shows general depression with loss of appetite but greatly increased thirst. An effective vaccine is now available.

Leptospirosis. A bacteria infection which attacks dogs in two ways according to the type of bacteria. One strain causes yellow jaundice which dogs may contract from rats, usually when rats have urinated in drinking water. The dog shows general depression, vomiting and intense thirst. There is also some infection of the eye and mouth membranes. It is very important to clear rats from the kennel area for this disease can often be fatal. Good cleaning and disinfection of the kennel area are essential. Another form of the bacteria produces less severe symptoms and recovery is usually within a few days. It is generally believed, however, that there is some damage to the kidneys which may be evident in later years. A vaccine to cover both types of infection is available.

Distemper and Hard-pad. Highly infectious, it would appear that the virus for both diseases is closely related. The dog will refuse food, have a heavy sleepy look, be shivering with an arched back and have a dry hot nose. In a few days a watery discharge will come away from eyes and nose. Although symptoms vary there may also be coughing and vomiting and the dog becomes quite prostrated. Isolation, warmth and a well ventilated kennel are essential. You must consult your veterinary surgeon without delay. Vaccines are available against both diseases. If a dog has been infected modern drugs and proper care and attention should avoid the worse complications but there is always the danger of some damage to the nervous system. The technical name for hard-pad is *epizootie encephalitis* (inflammation of the brain) so quiet and rest are most important.

Coccidiosis. I have only come across this parasite once and that was when a fairly large number of poultry was being housed near the kennels. The parasite appears to be similar to that which affects poultry causing diarrhoea and quite often with blood in the motions. Treatment requires the removal of the parasite from the intestine and very careful disinfecting of the kennels.

Tetanus. Most dogs are resistant to the infection which usually gains access to the system through a break in the skin surface. Once in the body it produces a poison which attacks the nervous system causing muscle spasms. The dog usually moves slowly and stiffly like a jointed toy. Proper treatment and nursing is usually effective. Some areas of the country are a much higher risk rate for infection than others and you will, no doubt, be aware of the potential local risk. You will know, of course, that it is now fairly common practice for humans to be given anti-tetanus injections after a dog bite or other fairly deep penetration of the flesh. It would, of course, be through a wound that your dog would become infected.

Apart from tetanus and jaundice I do not think that I have ever heard of a human being becoming infected with any of the diseases I have already mentioned. However, I do feel that at this particular point some mention should be made of rabies which is fatal for all animals and if transmitted to humans is disasterous. In this country we have been free from rabies as an endemic disease through the acceptance of importation and quarantine regulations. People surely cannot be ignorant of these regulations yet we read of cases of pets being smuggled through Customs for purely selfish reasons and with complete disregard for the serious problems that could develop.

The aim of the Ministry's rabies campaign is the protection of the human and farm animal population and the object of control was to stop the link from the animal side to the human side, where the results are horrific. The protection available from the use of vaccine has improved greatly and the latest vaccine, produced from cultured cells of human origin, have eliminated many of the secondary effects of previous vaccines. The disease has a long incubation period and should the disease become endemic, the post-exposure treatment and facilities required would be very costly.

There was a history of rabies in this country. An epidemic occurred from 1886 to 1903. There were over 3,000 cases of the disease, which was confined primarily to the dog population and did not spread into the wildlife except certain deer populations around cities (e.g. Richmond Park).

The disease was eliminated from the United Kingdom by ordering the muzzling and leashing of animals.

There was a small outbreak of the disease from 1918 to 1922 with 312 cases occurring in dogs. The outbreak was disturbing because the primary cause was not discovered.

In the last 50 years there have only been two cases of rabies (1969 to 1970) outside quarantine, with 27 cases of rabies occurring inside quarantine. The 10 human cases that have occurred in the United Kingdom were all infected abroad.

One of the two cases in 1969 to 1970 did have a wildlife implication and the risk of spread into wildlife was considered great enough to justify the action against the fox population in Surrey.

The public has been made more aware of the horrors of rabies due to increased publicity because they have an important part to play and it is necessary to maintain their interest for the risk to Britain is from animals coming from all over the world and not just Europe.

In an infected area the destruction of foxes would be ordered. This is necessary because the available evidence from the Continent suggests that the disease was probably all attributable to rabies in the fox. The disease is spread back from wildlife into domestic animals and although this is controlled to a large extent by vaccination it is not 100 per cent effective, (e.g. of the 27 cases of rabies occuring inside quarantine 60 per cent had been properly vaccinated).

The unrealiability of the vaccine means that quarantine is the best way to keep rabies out of an uninfected country.

An outbreak in the United Kingdom would be tackled in the first place on the domestic front, to try and stop it getting into wildlife. Only foxes would be destroyed and no other wildlife, unless it became implicated in the transmission of the disease. The control results of the French, who are using the same methods as would be used in the United Kingdom, show a big improvement.

It seems that not all foxes should be killed to reduce rabies. It was the view of ecologists, that the rabies situation had arisen because of an increase in the fox population, due for example to lack of predators. Experimental data has shown that if the fox population was reduced the infectivity of the virus runs itself out as the infected fox does not meet a sufficient number of non-infected foxes to spread the disease. In Britain we are particularly vulnerable as our fox population is very high.

A number of non-infectious conditions occur simply because a dog is a living creature and subject to the normal hazards of that state. As a working dog, however, the eye, nose, and ear are important and he will also come in contact with a number or numbers of internal and external parasites.

Eyes. A dog with a continually wet eye will most likely have a condition known as entropion. It is usually the lower lid which turns inward and causes irritation. Eventually it will damage the cornea and surgery is the only answer. I will deal with this later as a hereditary fault. Sometimes the eyelid turns outwards when the condition is known as ectropion. This obviously exposes the eye to foreign bodies. Surgery is the only remedy.

Grit, dirt or infection can lead to inflammation of the membrane. As in humans this state is known as conjunctivitis and ointment or eye drops will usually clear the inflammation. It sometimes happens that a dog will damage the sheen of the eye by scratching with a bramble and a bluish-white opaque will appear over the damaged area. This often leads to the growth of an ulcer on the cornea and the eye should be screened from any form of irritant whilst the ulcer is being treated. Eye lotions, antibiotics etc. are all helpful. I have found drops of best quality cod liver oil very effective. I would stress that it must be fresh and good quality.

Nose. The most common problem I have come across is cuts to the nose caused by brambles. Soothing ointments have been useful when I could stop the animal using its tongue to remove them. A blow on the nose may cause epistaxis (nose bleeding) and the normal remedies of cold packs and injections for persistant attacks are effective. There could be internal damage to the nasal membrane and this should always be checked. Inflammation of the membrane can occur and this will be noted first as a nasal discharge. Ointments should be used to prevent cracking and rawness in this sensitive area.

Ears. A very common cause of ear trouble arises from grass seeds, tiny pieces of straw or even small insects entering the ear canal. The irritation causes the dog to scratch and the base of the ear becomes very painful to touch. As the inflammation increases a nasty smelly area developes exuding a blackish-brown discharge. If not treated the ear canal becomes raw and ulcerated. The common name for this condition is canker which can extend into the middle ear creating infection there which requires treatment by sulphonamides and antibiotics. Regular attention to the ears is important. When my dogs have been out in the fields, especially in summer, I always comb the ears and inspect the ear canals when they return. If they have been in water I always dry the inside of the ear. Regular cleaning of the outer ear with swabs of cotton wool moistened with a mixture of methylated spirits and water is time well spent.

Parasites. The internal parasites common to dogs are several species of worms. Out in the country, and in kennel conditions, a dog has ample opportunity to pick up worm eggs. I try to avoid exercising my dogs on ground where sheep are grazing as this is a sure means of picking up eggs from the droppings.

Most dogs have **round worms** and these show in puppies that appear to be soft in condition and pot bellied. Puppies get worm eggs from their mother so it is a good idea to treat the bitch for round worms about three weeks before she is due to whelp. In adults is is not easy to check the condition unless there is a heavy infestation. Proprietary remedies are available but it is important to read the instructions very carefully.

It is the older dogs which usually have **tape worms**. Infestation is easy to check as segments of the worms can be seen in the excreta and around the dog's anus. Worming preparations are available for treating this variety of worm.

The most difficult to clear from the intestine are **hook** and **whip worms** which are resistant to all the normal worming medicines. The **hook worm**, as its name implies, hooks itself by the head to the wall of the intestine and unless the head can be released, the worm will continue to grow. There is now an effective treatment but fortunately these varieties are not all that common in this country. If these do occur, first treat the dog and then make sure that all the kennels have been scrupulously cleaned to destroy worm eggs and larvae. It may be that heat treatment is necessary for this last operation possibly involving the careful use of a blowlamp.

Summer and autumn are trying times for some of the external parasites such as **lice, fleas, harvest bugs** and **ticks**. Dogs ranging over grass where poultry and rabbits have been will soon pick up lice and fleas and an encounter with a hedgehog can be disasterous as these creatures are alive with fleas. Of course, these will bite the dog but will not live and breed on it. Dogs' fleas lay their eggs in dog bedding so it is essential to treat the sleeping quarters as well as the dog. Ticks come off sheep country and because they have barbed heads they are difficult to remove. If the tick is pulled away and the head left behind in the skin a nasty little infected sore will develop. Try using a lighted match or cigarette end held against the body of the tick. This will usually enduce the tick to retract the barbs on its head and the whole of the insect can be twisted free. Gammexine powder can be carefully rubbed into the coat to treat fleas and lice, but the most effective control for lice is a spray called Nuvan Top which can be obtained from your veterinary surgeon. It can also be used as a deterrent against fleas and lice after attending shows. Pay particular attention to the neck and base of the ears as lice can be very persistent.

Travel sickness and heat stroke. Whilst looking especially at problems arising from the nature of the Springer as a working dog or even as a show dog for that matter, we could well look at certain areas where we humans are directly responsible for illness and distress. Dogs that show symptoms of nervous stress when transported by car could well be given a sedative or tranquilliser before you start and this will ease the effects of travel sickness. I often see dogs transported to shows in extremely cramped conditions in mid-summer and there have been instances of dogs left locked in cars in the parking areas without any protection from the sun. A dog subjected to high temperatures like this can easily get heat stroke and it can be fatal. The only treatment you can use is to cool the body with cold water and attempt to give small quantities of saline solution through the mouth. Those of us who are connected with the management of large shows are very concerned about the number of dogs left in cars during hot weather and feel that much stronger action should be taken against people reported for this inhumane action. I have already mentioned the importance of shade for kennel runs.

Skin. Certain skin conditions are often the cause of anxiety and a properly balanced diet together with regular handling of the dog to check early symptoms of disorder will go a long way towards fending off serious trouble. The most unpleasant skin disorders are possibly the two forms of mange. They are common in most breeds of dog and the first known as **sarcoptic mange** is caused by a mite which causes intense itching. As the dog scratches and rubs there is loss of hair and the skin is thick and dry with a cracked surface. It is best to clip away any long hair and give medicated baths using some of the sulphur compounds. I have found Benzyl Benzoate Solution to be very effective for a variety of skin conditions. **Demodectic mange** is also caused by a mite but only certain blood lines appear to be vulnerable to this variety so it could well have an hereditary factor. Bald patches develop around the eyes and head and then spread to other areas. There is little scratching by the dog and the skin thickens and becomes covered with fine grey scales. New biotics are now available and the condition is seldom seen to-day, but isolation of infected animals and thorough cleaning and disinfection is essential. All bedding should be burnt. **Ringworm** can be passed to humans and care should be taken when dealing with cases of this skin disease. It is identified as small round patches, showing definite ring formation, when the hair is very thin or completely absent. The disease is also found in cattle and it may be that contact with troughs, fences etc. against which cattle have rubbed could be a source of infection. Antibiotics are available for treatment. **Eczema** and **Dermatitis** start, as in humans, with a small red patch which blisters and then breaks into raw wet areas over which a crust will form. Clip off the surrounding hair and dress with the usual preparations, that is antiseptics and drying powders. Eczema may be caused by an allergy so it is as well to look into this aspect.

Much disease is avoided by keeping the dog in good condition and a balanced diet must include protein, mineral and vitamin content. All the known vitamins are now obtainable in properly balanced tablet form. Mineral supplements are particularly helpful to the bitch while she is feeding puppies. Deficiencies of calcium, phosphorus and vitamin D will lead to **rickets**.

Diseases affecting the genital system are comparatively rare. Dogs do carry congenital faults such as **monorchidism** and **cryptorchidism** and whilst such dogs may be shown it is best not use them for breeding. Inflammation of the penis and sheath can be treated by douching the sheath with antiseptic or antibiotic solutions. This is perhaps a useful habit to adopt after the dog has been used at stud. As far as the bitches are concerned **ovarian cysts** are not uncommon and this might be the reason why a particular bitch was persistently producing false pregnancies. **Acute metritis** occurs if all the afterbirth is not cleared after whelping and the veterinary surgeon is needed urgently. In older bitches **chronic metritis** may occur and usually surgery is the only cure. The symptoms are usually thirst, lassitude, loss of appetite and quite often a pus-like discharge from the vulva.

Nephritis (*Kidney Disease*). This is common in older male dogs and there is no cure for the advanced stage. The disease is slow to take full effect but early stages are indicated by loss of appetitite, increased thirst and poor coat condition. Later there may be bad breath, vomiting and the animal becomes very weak. A condition known as **acute nephritis** may be caused by a number of factors any one of which may cause damage to the kidney tissues. The dog may well be in a state of collapse, in considerable pain and running a high temperature. The pulse is usually weak and fast and specific treatment is required. Inflammation of the bladder, known as **cystitis**, can be cured by treatment to kill the infection and by giving plenty of liquid to wash out the urinary system. The animal usually shows signs of pain when passing water. **Stones** sometimes form in the bladder and urethra and form an obstacle to the passing of water. An operation is necessary to remove the stones.

I have mentioned the advisability of handling your dogs regularly for in this way you will notice minor ailments and any physical damage they may have suffered. The following brief notes may be helpful as a guide to what you might be looking for at such times.

Growths. In old age tiny growths may be found on the body and in bitches on the mammary glands. These are usually benign and slow growers that can be removed by surgery. If the growths are malignant they will spread rapidly and there is no cure.

Mouth. Ulcers on tongue and cheek, may cause difficulty in eating and will be a cause of bad breath.

Teeth. Check for scaling. Occasionally this will develop very rapidly in hard limestone areas and a molar may be almost covered before you realise it. Gum infection is sure to set in and the tooth will have to be drawn. A bad tooth often leads to a swelling under the eye and, of course, feeding is painful.

Epulis. These are little fibrous growths at the meeting point of tooth and gum. Leave alone unless they are causing problems in which case the veterinary surgeon can remove them.

Tonsillitis. This is indicated by an inflamed throat and this may be part of another and more serious infection.

Gastritis. Springers will eat almost anything and this may well lead to an inflammation of the stomach which is followed by vomiting, increased thirst and some pain. I have had a number of problems with dogs that would swallow stones. Sometimes we were lucky and they were passed out with the motions but at other times operations have been necessary. Obviously an intestinal obstruction had been created.

Blockage in throat. It is not uncommon for a bone to become stuck in the throat or gullet and sometimes it is possible to withdraw it by hand from the mouth. This does need rapid attention as quite often the dog will panic and this creates a worse situation. I once lost a very promising youngster of about nine months of age who gulped a meat meal on a hot summer evening and lodged a piece of meat in the gullet. She immediately panicked and rushed around the kennel creating an even worse problem as the extended gullet pressed into the wind pipe and cut off her air supply. She was so strong and frantic that I could not get to her to massage the throat and in five minutes she was dead.

Anal glands. Quite often the anal glands become blocked and they can be opened by squeezing. If this is not done an abscess may form and the glands have to be removed by surgery. Anal tumours are seen in older dogs and if removed they do not usually grow again.

Anal and rectal prolapsis. This condition is usually caused by excessive straining when passing a motion. Puppies with a bad infestation of worms will over strain in an effort to clear the worms. Sometimes the condition will occur in older dogs when there has been a period of bad constipation that has not been noticed. Surgery is required to replace the prolapsis and insert stitches to keep it in place.

Hysteria. This is a local affection of the brain and may well be associated with bad diet or certain forms of poisoning. If uncertain the most helpful thing to do is to give sedatives until the veterinary surgeon has made a diagnosis. The use of feeding materials containing a very high percentage of white flour can cause this condition.

Paralysis. This indicates a damage to some part of the nervous system and it is best to keep the dog quiet and to seek professional advice.

Interdigital cysts. These are quite common and I once had one dog that was never free from them. They can be very painful and cause lameness. Bathing the affected area was helpful. This condition appears to be caused by blocked pores in the skin between the pads causing what appear to be blackheads. These should be gently squeezed out and the area painted with iodine. Regular attention must be given to this condition, throughout the dog's life, as the cysts recur. At the same time check the pads for thorns and grass seeds which seem to burrow their way under the skin and work their way up the leg.

Wounds. Check for all sorts of tears, bites and even shotgun pellet wounds. Long and deep wounds should be stitched but all should have the hair cleared around them and antiseptics used to clean the area before any dressing is placed on the wound. Sulphonamide antibiotic powder is a very useful thing to have in the kennel medicine chest. Our dogs have often been stung by wasps and bees. The bee sting should be squeezed out as quickly as possible. The area then needs bathing in a solution of bicarbonate of soda. The problem is more serious if the sting is on the tongue and the resulting swelling can easily cause a restriction in the throat. The bicarbonate solution can still be used as this will not have any ill effect on the dog if swallowed. A special mention ought to be made of snake bites. Although our only poisonous snake is the adder, a working dog in cover can get bitten. If this should happen try to cut across the bite and suck out the poison which is only dangerous if it is in the blood stream. Permanganate of potash makes a good first-aid dressing but an anti-snake serum injection should be given as soon as possible. A number of working dogs have died because effective treatment could not be given in time. Personally I would not work my dogs in an area known to harbour adders but left to their own devices dogs will wander and investigate. So if you take your pet into the country watch where he goes. Usually adder areas are signed as dangerous but damp swampy areas are always suspect.

I have left the subject of hereditary faults until last but not because I think them least important. Hereditary faults will appear in all species where breeding goes on and with present day general knowledge of simple genetics it is time that breeders of all dogs gave serious consideration to the possible outcome of their breeding programmes.

Too often a bitch is mated to a winning dog for no other reason than that he is winning or his line is producing current winners. Little consideration appears to be given to the faults on both sides and how these will be reflected in the off-spring. Most animals with the faults I will mention show signs of them and refusal to breed from such stock is likely to help to eradicate the defects. There must be frankness about affected dogs and a willingness to admit their unsuitability for breeding.

Entropion. I have already made brief mention of this condition and there is little doubt that it exists in certain blood lines in English Springers. The eyelids are turned inwards towards the eyeball and both eyes may be affected. In less severe cases the irritation set up by the brushing of the eyelashes against the surface of the cornea produces discomfort and a great deal of fluid which cannot be dealt with by the tear ducts. This excessive fluid overflows and runs down the side of the face. Use of ointments etc. has no effect on the condition which will gradually worsen. So many weird and outlandish explanations have been offered that they are quite unbelievable. In more severe cases the inturning is such that the hard rim of the eyelid rubs against the cornea and this leads to bruising and inflammation which will show up on the cornea as a pale milky blue patch. The varying condition is, of course, dependent on the amount of eyelid that is inturned. If only in the corner of the eye the effect is less severe but if the whole length of the lid is inturned then the condition causes constant pain and discomfort and will eventually cause blindness. Early recognition is important for then surgery can be used to correct the condition and some veterinary surgeons have become very skilled at this particular and rather delicate operation. It could well be that other eye problems have led you to believe incorrectly that your dog has Entropion but I am fairly confident that the condition is reasonably easy to recognise and I would recommend very early consultation with your veterinary surgeon. I have been breeding dogs since the 1930s and judging at Championship Show level for many years and I never cease to be amazed at comments made to me by some exhibitors in an effort to cover up a fault in their dog. Not so long ago I was looking very carefully at the eyes of an Old English Sheepdog that had been brought under me in a Variety Class. The eye lacked pigmentation and the exhibitor explained this by saying that she was sorry about the eye but the dog had bumped into the wheelbarrow the previous day and knocked off the pigmentation! What hope have we got of dealing with hereditary diseases if this is the standard of knowledge of some of our breeders?

Progressive retinal atrophy. This condition is usually referred to as P.R.A. or sometimes as 'night blindness'. The nerve cells comprising the retina at the back of the eyeball waste away giving impaired vision. In due course the dog becomes totally blind. It was during late evening and at night that people first noticed that their dogs were bumping into objects and so detected signs of defective vision. Hence the description of 'night blindness' was given. The earlier symptoms are an increase in the size of the eye pupil and at certain times a red or green glow can be seen in the eye. As the loss of sight increases the dog becomes less sure of its movements in unfamiliar surroundings and whilst moving objects may be seen in clear light a static object may not be seen at all. Dogs trained to the gun may not mark their game or may even become lost when returning with a bird to a handler who is standing still or partially in cover. There is no discharge of water from the eye and it is not a painful disease but quite often cataracts develop and these are recognised as cloud or milky patches on the eyeball. There is no treatment.

P.R.A. is known to be hereditary to man and other animals. It has been recorded as present in English Springers. This is a condition that can be controlled by breeders who must surely realise that every dog/bitch that has produced a blind puppy must carry a gene for the defect even though it has normal sight itself. There is, therefore, the possibility that the condition will be passed on again to future litters. In some breeds, for instance the Irish Setter, the condition can be diagnosed at puppy stage but in other breeds it may not show until the dog is adult and complete blindness may not occur until quite late in life. Hence many owners have not suspected a defect and simply regarded it as a part of old age. Accurate diagnosis of P.R.A. can be made by examining the eye with an opthalmoscope. This instrument may detect the presence of pigment spots or narrowing blood vessels on the retina. The presence of either indicates atrophy of the retina. Many breeders are now having their stock checked and a number of Breed Clubs arrange for mass checks to be carried out at their shows. Stock declared free may be recorded at the Kennel Club, under arrangements made between them and the British Veterinary Association.

Canine hip Dysplasia. The normal hip is a ball and socket joint and hip dysplasia is the name given to any abnormal development of that joint in the dog. The socket part of the joint, formed by the junction of the three pelvis bones, is a cup-shaped cavity lined with cartilage and into this the rounded head of the thigh bone (known as the femur and also covered with cartilage) fits making a tight but freely moving joint. The nature of the joint is such that it gives rotary movement and the two parts of the joint are kept in place by strong fibrous ligaments. Many breeds of dog, especially the larger ones, have faulty conformation of this joint and occurrence is world wide.

As a result of research into the condition there is little doubt that the defect is controlled by hereditary factors. Presence of the disease will be noticed from poor movement in the hind legs which shows weakness and lack of driving power. There is also a tendency to excessive sideways movement of the pelvis and hips when the dog is moved at a slow pace. Dogs will tire easily during exercise and will often sit far more than usual. In extreme cases a clicking noise in the hip joint may be heard as the dog moves or if the hind legs are manipulated. Sometimes movement of the thigh towards the mid-line of the dog will cause the head of the femur to slip out of the socket and a reverse movement of the leg will cause the head of the femur to slip back into place with a snap. It may happen that the head of the femur will come completely out of the socket whilst the dog is moving or even lying down. This will cause severe pain until the head is manipulated back into place. X-ray examination is necessary to determine any abnormality and only those dogs which show complete freedom should be used for breeding purposes. It must be stressed that the interpretation of the X-ray plate requires a great deal of skill and experience and I recommend that you use the Kennel Club Scheme. Your veterinary surgeon should be able to give you full details. Remember, if his diagnosis is positive you should be withdrawing a dog from stud or withdrawing a brood bitch from your breeding programme.

The mouth and teeth. I feel that no work dealing with some hereditary faults should avoid mention of the mouth and teeth. The Standard states that the Springer should have strong jaws with a regular and complete scissor bite, i.e. the upper teeth closely overlapping the lower teeth and set at right angles to the jaws. There are instances of undershot or overshot mouths, that is where the bottom jaw is longer than the top jaw or vice versa. In these circumstances a scissor bite is an impossibility. The condition does not cause any discomfort to the dog. In the trial dog a badly undershot jaw may be a hinderance in retrieving. It is an hereditary fault and dogs with this defect should not be used for breeding. A show dog with this fault should be penalised and only placed in very exceptional circumstances.

In Chapter 9 I will mention the hard mouthed dog and the penalty it will pay at trials. Miss Hooper, who knew so much about both Show and Working Springers always maintained that this was also an hereditary fault and she based her theory on its occurrence in certain blood lines.

8 Showing, Stewarding and Judging

The important introduction to showing has, I suppose, taken place when you choose your first puppy. You will, of course, have made your purchase from blood lines which reflect your reason for buying and so even the 'pet' puppy becomes an object for comparison with others of his kind. A great deal of pleasure can be had by showing your dog and along with this considerable knowledge of the breed begins to build up from conversations with the many people you will meet. A word of warning—beware of the newcomers who overnight have become authorities on the breed.

Your puppy must have been trained in ring craft and you should practise walking him up and down on a slack lead. Never string a gundog up by his neck on the lead in the manner in which terriers are shown. Train him to stand well on his own and this can be achieved with a short time spent each day until you have accustomed him to what you

Miss Janet Shaw's
Sh. Ch. Ardencote
Tapestry.

want. Some puppies learn more quickly than others but you will need patience. A puppy can be shown from the age of six months upwards and I always start training mine to stand as soon as they are walking around the kennel. Of course, the walking up and down comes a little later say about sixteen weeks old but do not over do it. A short training time each day is the best method. Some blood lines in English Springers mature much earlier than others and quite often a good puppy will be placed lower down the line than the winner simply because it lacks maturity. So do not rush into showing, wait until you feel that your puppy is ready and will be able to attain the placing he deserves. Try and avoid 'topping and tailing' your puppy, that is over-handling by holding head and tail, with legs arranged and neck outstretched with handler kneeling or stooping beside it. It is always helpful in the early stages to stand your puppy in front of a long mirror as you can then see what the judge will be seeing. In the same way, if you move the mirror into the garden you will also have the Judge's view of your puppy's movement. The grand master of standing and showing a dog was the late H. S. Lloyd, owner of the famour *of Ware* prefix. Never do I recall him 'topping and tailing' a dog. Of course he spent many hours in the training process but his dogs were a pleasure to watch in the show ring.

Choose your first show fairly carefully. Often there is no benching and all the dogs have to lie on the floor quite close together and this is quite a strain on a young puppy especially if many of the other breeds are noisy. A benched show is often a less harrowing experience. Sanction and limited shows usually cater for variety classes, that is classes where all breeds are mixed and entry is governed only by age and previous wins. The open and general championship shows cater for most popular breeds where dogs are only in competition with their own breed or variety. Then there are the Breed Club shows where only one breed may be exhibited. It is not easy to tell the beginners where to enter but if you are sure of yourself or your dog I would suggest that you enter for a sanction show, or an open show of a Breed Club where entry fees will be lower. Choose a show where the judge is an established and well known 'all rounder' or is established and respected in your own breed. If you do not get an award, you always have the opportunity of asking the judge's opinion after the show. Entry fees for championship shows are expensive, and likely to increase, so buy your early experience as cheaply as you can.

All the shows are advertised in the weekly dog papers so you should be able to find a show not too far from home. You will also find notes on your breed in the papers and as your interest grows you will be able to keep in touch with the major trends in your breed and the Breed Club activities.

Having selected the show, write to the show secretary for a schedule which will include an entry form and tell you all you need to know about entering your dog. It always helps to send your request on a post card as it saves the secretary having to open an envelope and for the larger shows it means that your schedule arrives more quickly. Most secretaries work in an honorary capacity and give a great deal of their time to the dog fancy; please do not ring at midnight or in the middle of Sunday lunch. As a show secretary I know how annoying this can be and it is really quite unnecessary and very inconsiderate.

Your schedule and entry form have arrived and you can now choose your classes. Try and select a class that is appropriate to the age and experience of your dog. Entering a puppy in an Open Class is usually only a waste of money. Your entry form should be completed carefully and all sections completed. Please use BLOCK LETTERS where this is requested. It is a tremendous help to the secretary and the printer when the catalogue is being prepared. I know only too well the amount of time and energy that is wasted in trying to decipher names of owners and names of dogs. You should also remember that mistakes on entry forms, especially incorrect names of dogs, may lead to disqualification later and the cancellation of any award that may have been won.

The closing date for entry is always given on the schedule and the postmark must not show a later date. So always post in good time but before posting check all details and make sure you have enclosed the entry fees. I have received many entry forms without fees which means that they have had to be returned and on occasions I have received entry fees with a completely blank entry form.

After posting your entry you have to ensure that your dog is properly prepared for his arrival on the day. It seems that so many dogs are bundled into cars at the last minute and on arrival at the show there is a frantic rush to complete preparation of the coat. This usually results in a poor finish and piles of dead hair left at the venue which causes immense problems for the show management. Indeed many venues have been lost because of the inconsiderate behaviour of certain exhibitors.

The Springer's coat needs regular and thorough brushing and combing because of the dense undercoat. The brushing and combing will bring out the dead hair and leave the top-coat lying straight and smooth. Any dead or faded hair left on the head, ears and flank should be 'plucked' using finger and thumb. If this is done correctly and carefully it does not hurt the dog but a little patience is necessary until you develop the technique.

Never use scissors, clippers or a knife as it will ruin the coat. It is sad to see so many Springers in the ring to-day that have obviously been prepared with clippers; sometimes with a razor to shave behind the ear and down the neck. I am strongly of the opinion that this form of preparation should be penalised by judges. Curved scissors may be used to trim the hair round the shape of the foot. A great deal of hair grows between the toes and this should be trimmed to match the line around the pads. Hair underneath the foot should also be trimmed back to the pads. Excess hair here allows matting and soil clogs into little hard balls which can produce sore feet and lead to lameness. Any long hair at the back of the front leg should be trimmed at the bottom for about an inch according to the length of the leg. In the same way, hair on the back legs from below the hock to the foot should be trimmed close to the leg.

Toenails rarely need cutting if the dog has a reasonable amount of exercise on hard surfaces. There may be excess growth if the dog is always exercised on grass, in which case a pair of dog nail cutters should be used. Always take care not to cut the quick which shows as a darker colour through the nail. Any rough edges can be smoothed down using an ordinary nail-file or a small electrician's file.

I would not recommend that your Springer had a regular bathing routine. A good swim in a clean river, stream or pond in the summer should be quite sufficient. However, dogs kept in urban areas where the polluted atmosphere tends to lay down a deposit on the ground may well benefit from a bath at reasonable intervals. Before you put your dog in the bath, plug his ears with cotton wool so that water cannot get into the inner ear. After using a good dog shampoo rinse the coat well with clean, warm water. Rubbing down with a chamois leather will dry the coat and leave a very nice finish. I have always found that a good deep bed of clean oat straw keeps the coat clean and in a lovely shiny condition. Always beware of barley straw which can cause a condition which looks like sarcoptic mange as some dogs appear to have an allergy to this type of straw.

Bringing dirty dogs into the show ring will not enhance their chances of winning and it is not exactly a complimentary gesture towards the judge.

If you travel to the show by car remember that your dog may not be a good traveller. Like some human beings he may suffer from carsickness. You have spent a lot of time getting him ready so try to ensure that he arrives clean and dry. A large sheet tied around the neck will catch the dribble and keep his neck and legs clean. Newspapers help to soak up the wet but beware of the printers' ink on his nice white markings!

Some human remedies for seasickness may be tried but make sure of the ingredients so that they are suitable for dogs. I found that it was best to get a puppy into a car as soon as possible at first for short journeys and then gradually increase the distance. Mostly I found that the dogs enjoyed the car but to one or two it has always been the boring prelude to a show.

I think the exception is the working dog which having been taken shooting once or twice, relates the car ride to the pleasure of the hunt. The gun being taken from the rack for cleaning can give the same stimulation.

Take all you need at the show in a handy bag—a small towel, drinking bowl, spare lead, brush, comb and hand-glove. If you are going to a benched show you will need a bench chain and bench rug as well as a show lead. A small container of water, perhaps milk for a puppy, is always useful as it may not be easy to find the water supply at the show. A supply of food should not be necessary but a small quantity can always be taken for a puppy. At the larger championship shows there are trade stands where you can always make emergency purchases. A few 'Vetsyme' tablets, a piece of dry cooked meat or a rabbit's foot held in your closed hand will always keep your dog attentive in the ring. Remember your exhibitor's pass if one has been sent to you.

Try to arrive at the show in good time as it allows your dog time to settle down especially if he has not travelled too well. If it is a benched show, find your bench and make your dog comfortable and see that he is offered a drink of water. Make sure you know where your judging ring is situated and when your class is likely to be due and be at the ringside well before you are needed.

The steward will give you your ring number when your class is called and it is always helpful if you can tell him your number. Keep your dog interested and try to make sure that he shows to best advantage. You entered for the judge's opinion so please accept his awards with good grace. Unfortunately there are frequent examples of very bad manners in the ring these days. If you gain an award in your first class, or even if unplaced, stand in the order of your award on the side of the ring for dogs already seen when it comes to your next class.

There are days when you will be delighted and days when you will be disappointed. Remember your dog has his good days and days when he is just a little bit off colour. Just like humans in fact. So if he wins one day it does not necessarily follow that he should win automatically the next.

You will be proud of your Prize Cards and will undoubtedly be looking to the day when you collect your first 'Green Card', that elusive Challenge Certificate offered by the Kennel Club at the championship shows. Three of these awarded by three different judges and you have made up your first Show Champion. You must now get some real training done for it should be your ambition to gain a 'Qualifier' with your dog which will entitle him to the title of

Champion. The Qualifier is not difficult. Your dog has to satisfy two appointed Field Trial judges that he has hunting instincts and will retrieve. It is not essential that he should be steady to shot but how much better if he is! Surely in a breed like ours that has its ancestory steeped in the working side, it should not be impossible for our dogs to display hunting instincts and to be trained to retrieve. After some twenty-five years as Secretary to the parent breed Club I am convinced that the introduction of the 'Show Champion' status was detrimental to the breed as a whole.

It is impossible to run a show without ring stewards and good ring stewards are worth their weight in gold! Stewarding for a good judge is an excellent way to get to know a breed and most show secretaries will be only too pleased to accept your offer of help. You have to learn how to be a good steward so for your first show ask to be placed with an experienced steward who will be able to show you how to go about the job. If you do not mention your inexperience you could find yourself stewarding single handed in a fairly large entry of a breed completely unknown to you.

About a week before the show, the secretary of the show will send you an admission ticket and a car park label together with a note of the breed(s) for which you will be stewarding and the times at which judging will commence. The smaller shows may not do this but it would be usual for the secretary to send you a schedule which will give you all the important details you will need.

Allow plenty of time for your journey and try to arrive on the show ground at least half-an-hour before judging of your breed(s) is due to commence. Report your arrival to the secretary, or the chief steward at a large show, and collect your steward's box or bag which should contain a catalogue, exhibitors's ring numbers, prize cards and any other paper work which will be necessary in the ring. Check the location of your ring and try to arrive there in good time to get the judge's table, chairs and award board and to get your own paper work in order and ready for the first class. It is always useful to take your own award card which you mark from class to class. This allows you to check unbeaten exhibits and helps you in the placing of later classes.

If another steward has been allocated to your ring it is important for you both to decide on a division of the duties. At a championship or large open show it is helpful to know where your breed is benched and to check the benches against your catalogue to note the probable absentees.

When the judge arrives at the ring, introduce yourself as his steward and ask whether he requires the dogs to be brought into the ring in any particular way.

Now you can call in the first class and check those present against the entries in the catalogue and give each exhibitor the correct ring number. Advise the judge of any absentees so that he can make a note in his judging book. The steward should now retire to the ring table or elsewhere so that he is quite unobtrusive yet always available when he is wanted by the judge.

When the judge has placed his winning dogs he will sometimes call the steward and tell him that he is finished with the remaining exhibits. The steward can then relay the judge's comment in a pleasant and friendly manner. Remember that these exhibitors will be disappointed and a pleasant approach by the steward is conducive to good ring atmosphere and behaviour. While the judge is marking his book, the steward can give out the prize cards and it is usual for the numbers of the exhibits to be called in a strong voice for the benefit of ringside spectators. Enter these numbers on your own award card and make sure to collect the slip(s) from the judge's book after the judge has completed his notes. Whilst the judge is examining the dogs in the next class, it should be possible for you to check the markings on the judging slip against your own award card. This is most helpful and can be done without upsetting or annoying the judge. Errors on award slips cause a great deal of trouble to the secretary after the show.

Now call in the second class, placing new dogs on one side of the ring and those that the judge has already seen on the opposite side. You can ask the judge whether he would like his 'seen' dogs placed in order of his previous awards. Most judges prefer this to be done but some do not so it is always advisable to ask. This is where your own award card will be useful and as the judge progresses through his classes it will save a great deal of time and frustration. Ultimately, of course, it is the judge's responsibility to remember his previous placings.

In the specimen shown below the steward can see immediately which dogs have met and as each dog is beaten it is crossed off leaving the unbeaten exhibits clearly identifiable. These numbers can then be given to the judge if he wishes to have them brought into the ring when deciding on the Best of Sex and Best of Breed.

No. Class	Sex	Ist	2nd	3rd.	Res.	V.H.C.	H.C.
1	D	72	68	54	80	73	56
2	D	79	72	68	49	36	56
3	D	86	72	49	50	68	56
4	B	55	73	69	54	57	61
5	B	63	73	67	54	61	62
6	B	82	63	73	61	84	90

Many exhibitors are under the impression that they have a 'right' to challenge for a certificate at a championship show and quite often the exhibit placed second in Open Dog, although not an unbeaten exhibit, will be brought into the ring to challenge. This is entirely at the discretion of the judge.

The steward should be very careful to check his unbeaten dogs and to be able to give the judge accurate information when asked. The judge is at liberty to ask for any dog to be brought into the ring and to award the certificate as he pleases. He is at liberty to change his mind and reverse a decision but this is not a popular move with exhibitors. As a steward it is possible to see the exhibits at close quarters, have a better view of their movement and watch the judge's handling techniques. This is not easy from the ringside and accounts for a great deal of the 'ringside judging' comments that one hears from some of the spectators. Try and pick your own winners in each class and compare them with the final placings of an experienced judge. The day may come when you want to be a judge. How do you arrive in the middle of the ring?

On the Continent there are formal training schemes for judges. Here you respond to an invitation and if you accept you will have debated in your mind whether you are competent to do the job. I know a number of very experienced people who do not feel able to judge and many others who never appear to be invited. So how do you become a judge? Anyone may judge at a sanction, limited or open show—all you need is the invitation. One can only hope that show committees are careful in their selection and pay attention to a prospective judge's experience in the breed or group of breeds that he will be invited to judge. A good judge has an eye for a dog and will be quite competent to judge most breeds and, like everything else, a great deal comes with experience. Some judges will never be really good no matter how many classes and breeds they judge but the judgement of those with ability will be respected and their services will always be in demand. At the moment there is a dearth of promising and up-and-coming all-rounders and each year takes its toll of those who are currently household names in 'dogdom'.

At the breed and general championship shows, the Kennel Club allocates its own challenge certificates which count towards the title of champion and show champion. An invitation to judge at one of these shows is subject to approval of the Kennel Club and the nominee judge's qualifications will be considered very carefully.

A first judging appointment will be a demanding decision to most people. One is very conscious of the responsibility and the fact that in awarding a high prize one is placing a mark of merit on that particular exhibit. Of course you may make a mistake, most judges will have done so and the better ones will be willing to admit it. The experience of a mistake and the reasoning afterwards will make them all the better later on.

A judge should be at the show on time, reporting first to the secretary and then to his ring. A prompt start to judging is always appreciated; it allows the show to run smoothly and exhibitors should not be kept waiting without very good reason. Each dog should be examined carefully even though at first glance you may realise that it is a very inferior representative of its breed. Each exhibitor has paid the same entry fee and is entitled to the same degree of consideration. Do try and be gentle when you handle the dogs. Nothing is more off-putting especially for a young puppy at its first show, than rough handling by a judge especially when the mouth is being examined. Once judging has commenced, the judge's full and complete concentration should be given to that task. As an exhibitor I have often been annoyed when a judge has interrupted judging in the middle of class to speak to a friend passing by or standing at the ringside. Animated and lengthy talk between judge and exhibitor is not desirable as it can be misinterpreted but I cannot see why a pleasant 'Good Morning' etc. is out of place, especially when, at the breed shows, judge and many exhibitors are extremely well known to each other. It is unfortunate that there are people around who are only too willing to put the wrong interpretation on the most innocent of situations. So having made sure that your own attitude and behaviour has been impeccable do not tolerate rudeness and bad ring behaviour from the exhibitors. There is far too much of that today and it is giving the dog fancy quite the wrong public image. Insulting behaviour should be reported to the Kennel Club when it can be investigated and dealt with effectively. I feel quite strongly that judges should also be far more strict on bad temperament in the dogs they are judging, especially in gundogs. A gundog that is aggressive could not be taken out for a day's shooting with confidence.

Completion of the judging book is important especially when challenge certificates are on offer. A good steward will always keep his eye on this and make sure that the correct exhibitor's numbers are entered and that the appropriate slip from the book reaches the secretary's office. When judging is finished some of the exhibitors may wish to say 'Thank you' for the award(s) you have given their dog; others may want to ask you why you did not give their dog any award at all. You must try to be honest about your reply but the honesty needs to be tempered with tact and kindness especially for those exhibitors at their first show with their first dog. These people need encouragement for they may become great breeders and enthusiasts in the years to come. Of course, you may have to face an aggressive exhibitor who demands to know why his dog did not get an award. Once again, you give an honest reply and one that is not calculated to engender more aggression. Your own integrity and the respect of exhibitors as a whole, will soon deter the troublemakers but a 'first time' judge is often fair game for some of these people.

Ought you to charge a fee? If so, how much? There are many opinions about this and I am sure that no judge should be expected to be out-of-pocket and should, at least, be offered travelling costs. As a show secretary I realise the problem from both sides. The show must pay its way and make a reasonable profit to cover possible future losses but the judges must also have a fair deal as many of them will have done a hard day's work. Generally, I feel that the newer and less experienced judges should not expect the remuneration of the established top judges. In fact I find many of the top ranking judges less demanding than some of the newer faces. Really you decide on the personal expenses incurred, the amount of work you will have to do and suggest a fee accordingly. Show secretaries will soon tell you if they feel it is too expensive. Of course, a judge may need more experience in a particular breed and will often give services free of charge in order to gain that experience. Breed Clubs will always know of reliable people who fit into this category, but it is as well perhaps to consider the capabilities and perhaps motives of those whose services are too freely offered but not supported by any degree of experience in any particular breed.

9   Training and Working

The Springer is the general purpose gun dog for it can hunt, put up the game and retrieve whilst working through thick cover and in water. As was mentioned in Chapter 4 there must be hundreds of Springers that are used just for this purpose, with no thought of entering either for Shows or Field Trials. Here I would like to quote the late Mr William Arkwright (whose daughter Angela was later to become Lady Lambe and President of the English Springer Spaniel Club) who was of the opinion that a Spaniel had to have four natural qualities which he listed as (1) Docility (2) Courage (3) Nose (4) Style. Mr Arkwright was clear in his own mind that such natural qualities were hereditary and I have no doubt at all in my own mind that this must be true. How can you tell whether your dog has these instincts? A docile dog shows a wish to please his owner and has an enquiring look and a sort of 'what am I to do next expression?' that I find hard to explain but is easy to see. I believe this can be seen in quite a young puppy. A headstrong dog is very difficult and I know now that I have wasted a lot of time with the wrong blood lines. A dog needs courage to face thick cover but if the instinct is there he can be encouraged. So often I have seen dogs taken for qualifying certificates who were just not interested. A dog with a good nose is interested in really hunting out his neighbourhood and not just in selecting the best spot on which to pass his motions. Again I have seen dogs taken for qualifiers that might just as well have been out for a Sunday afternoon stroll. Style I am convinced is hereditary—it just puts the finishing touches to a job that has been done in quite a satisfactory manner and has now had the polish put on. Again perhaps not too easy to describe but we all know what it is. We see it in so many of life's activities and know just what a difference it makes. However, you may have bought a Springer for a pet and feel that all this does not really concern you. Even for your Springer some simple training will be valuable and, I would suggest, an important feature of his early life. No matter what his life style he should be obedient and some early obedience work will help to ensure that he walks to heel on a lead. So often you see the dog from next door taking its owner for a walk! You can start quite early with a puppy on a lead. Some will not take to it very well at first but it will come with patience. It is better to use what is known as a 'slip lead' rather than a collar and separate lead and then when the puppy pulls forward he can be pulled gently but firmly back to you with the command 'heel'. A very fine mesh chain choke collar is perhaps better than a slip lead but a lot depends upon your puppy. Remember that whilst you must be firm you must also be kind. If you live in the country it is very important that your dog should be used to livestock and it is a good idea to walk young stock on a lead through sheep, cattle and poultry pulling them back with a firm 'no' every time they show any interest in chasing. Your dog will usually respond to this training and eventually walk with you, off the lead, in complete safety, but I would recommend that he be made to walk at heel. Living in the country I am still amazed to see cars draw up in a field entrance for a picnic on Saturday or Sunday and the dog turned loose to roam at will. At lambing season and at other times of the year this is a great temptation for a dog and can be an expensive business for the farmer and possibly the owner of the dog.

These early stages of obedience are quite easy to do at home but if you really do not feel competent then you will be able to find a Training Society fairly near. There are a great many offering training classes nowadays and the secretary of your nearest Canine Society should be able to help you make contact. Whilst the training to walk to heel is going on it will be easy to combine the command 'sit'. As you walk along with the puppy on a lead make a number of irregular stops, give the command 'sit' and press your puppy to the 'sit' position by pressure on his buttocks with your hand. Repeat the pressure every time he tries to get up. After a time he will learn to sit without the pressure of your hand. Once you have completed this stage you can try 'sit and stay'; that is make your puppy sit and give the command 'stay' using a raised hand signal. Walk away a very short distance and then turn and watch your puppy. If he has moved and tried to follow you take him back to where you sat him down and give another very firm command to 'sit and stay' perhaps enforcing the command with the pressure of your hand on his buttocks. After a time he will learn to sit and stay on command. Your puppy must now be encouraged to return directly to you on the command 'come' accompanied by an encouraging pat on your leg. Having returned to you your puppy should sit. Do not overdo the training sessions, a little at a time at regular intervals each day is the best method and of course it is most important that the puppy should be praised for doing a task properly and so his natural instinct to please will be satisfied. It is quite easy to train the puppy to respond to the whistle and to introduce little bits of training at feeding time when the puppy can be expected to sit before being fed. The basic training I have described so far can, and in my opinion, should be given to all dogs. It helps them to live in the community without being

a nuisance and source of annoyance to their owners and other people. At the same time it is an activity to help develop their intelligence. I have always believed that, whilst the basic intelligence factor may be there, there needs to be contact with human beings and some form of mental activity in order to develop the basic fact.

If you are contemplating a show career for your puppy all the basic training I have mentioned so far will be valuable. The contact with other dogs at training classes is a good experience for a puppy and gets it used to moving around in mixed company. It also helps those who are a little shy of early contacts and helps to give them confidence. Also very important, of course, is that it allows the owner to handle and show his dog to full advantage. Some people will not train their dogs to sit believing this to be detrimental in the show, but at the same time

Hartshorn Ruby owned and bred by Mrs M. A. Stephens participating in a trial in Norfolk which she won. She has just flushed a pheasant and is marking its fall.

your dog can be taught to stand and this is a great help.

The training given so far is equally valuable as a preparation for work in the field and what I shall write from now on is purely a system that I have worked out for myself. I was determined that my Springers should work but always realised that my best efforts would not produce the speed and style of the field trial blood lines. I read the books and I talked to the professional trainers and handlers and had tremendous help and guidance from them all. I am appreciative of the support of Miss Francis and for that extra 'ability' that the introduction of the Higham blood line gave to my own stock.

The pure obedience work may have been commenced at three or four months of age. It will really depend upon your puppy but after the obedience stage I usually begin the training for the retrieve. Most Springers take naturally to retrieving and so there should not be any great difficulty with this part of the work. You will need a 'dummy' but these need not be anything very special. Quite often I have used a stick, an old sock stuffed with rags, an old fur glove or an old rabbit skin stuffed and stitched. Whatever you use at this stage should not be heavy but light enough for the puppy to carry easily in its mouth. Put your puppy in the 'sit' position and show him the dummy making sure that he becomes interested in it. It may be necessary to have a restraining hand on the collar at this stage. Repeat your command to 'sit' and making sure that the puppy has his attention on the dummy throw it a short distance in front of him. As you throw, keep a restraining hand on the puppy and give a firm command of 'no' when he tries to go forward. Now make sure that he sits and watches the dummy for a short interval, then give the command 'fetch' or 'bring' and let him go. Once he has picked up the dummy encourage him to return directly to you either by using the whistle or the command 'come' perhaps with the extra encouragement of patting the side of your leg. When you use the whistle for training remember you will need to use two notes. One for stopping and sitting your dog at a distance and another for the recall. The note used for stopping should be given at the same time as the combined 'sit' and raised hand signal. Most gundog people seem to favour the word 'hup' instead of 'sit' so at some of your early obedience classes you may be concerned to hear these two words used as commands for the same purpose. Always use the same words of command and do not overdo the exercise. Three or four times is sufficient. Try to finish in a successful retrieve so that the puppy can be praised but as soon as his interest wains stop the exercise and give him a rest. On his retrieves make sure that he delivers the dummy to your hand and does not drop it on the ground in front of you. It is important at this stage that you remember never to chase your puppy if he wants to play with the dummy and run away with it.

If you do he will think it all part of a game and continue to be elusive. Just walk away and his natural instinct is for him to come to you with the dummy. Once this has been mastered you can try a hidden retrieve. You will need some help as, while somebody else holds your puppy at the sit on a lead, you trail the dummy along the ground on a length of cord and eventually leave it behind a bush or in thick grass, but out of sight. Go back to your puppy and release him with an encouraging 'hi lost' giving an arm direction towards the dummy. He may not go far and will look back for help. Encourage again and eventually he should take up the ground scent and find the dummy. Once he has found it, encourage his return with the whistle or 'good dog' walking backwards away from him so that he delivers directly to your hand. As always give encouragement for a job well done.

Your puppy must not be gun-shy and so it is advisable to get him used to loud noises and bangs. However when you do this make sure that the noise is in the vicinity of the puppy but not so close that he is frighened. Miss Hooper told me that she used to blow up paper bags and then burst them, after which she showed them to the puppies so that they could see that they were harmless. Training pistols that fire blanks, an airgun or a .410 shotgun are all useful at this stage, but never at close range until you are absolutely sure that your puppy will not be upset. Personally I do not like the training pistols and a few of my dogs, whilst having no fear of the .410 or 12 bore, were always a little apprehensive of the training pistol. Always fire whatever weapon you have for training when the dog is some distance in front of you. Once this hurdle has been overcome you can go to the next stage. It is not a bad idea to take a youngster to a shoot, not for him to be in the way, but to get used to the noise and in particular the gunfire. You can now try to teach the direction which you want the dog to hunt by throwing the dummy in that direction, at the same time indicating the direction with your other arm and giving 'hi lost'. If this is repeated with patience your dog will stop to your whistle and look to you for direction and then follow your left or right arm direction as the case may be. At this stage try and get cold game for the retrieve. Pheasant may not be so easy, or even rabbit in some areas, but pigeons are certainly readily obtainable and quite satisfactory. When I was having problems with cold game, my husband used to shoot starlings and we used those. One of the professionals had told me that the starling has the right kind of smell and it was certainly a useful tip. The dogs did not like crows or rooks and in these early stages it was encouragement that they needed. This more serious side of the training will begin when the dog is about eight months old. It will be all that much easier if the very early and simple obedience work has been properly learned. A number of Gundog Societies now run working tests with novice and advanced tests. Attendance at these is all very helpful; it gets your dog acclimatised to the working scene and gives you an opportunity to see other people's successes, and failures, and to talk over your training problems with other people. Many of our best known trainers and handlers give their time to these working tests and I have always found them willing to be constructive and helpful.

At some stage you will need to teach your dog to 'quarter' across his ground. This can be done by walking along with your dog at heel and dropping the dummy so that the dog does not see it fall. Carry on for a short distance and then send your dog back with the usual 'hi lost'. If this is first done with the wind coming towards you the dog will scent the dummy more easily and the distance of the retrieve can be considerably increased. The next stage is to drop the dummy in such a position that when the dog is sent out the wind is blowing with him and he does not have the advantage of the scent being carried to him. In this way the dog will have to hunt from side to side until it gets wind of the dummy. Quite often a dog will pause and look for help, in which case a left or right signal will send him off in the right direction.

Of course I have covered quickly several months of work during which your patience will have been sorely tried on many occasions. However, if you have been keeping more than one puppy you will have realised fairly early on which was showing most promise. Obviously if there is no response to the obedience training, if there is complete refusal to retrieve or a marked tendency to shyness of gunshot, then you are better giving your time and attention to another puppy.

You can also teach quartering by hunting your dog slightly in front of you. At fairly regular intervals attract its attention with the whistle (do not use the 'sit' or 'recall' notes) and then change direction left to right and vice versa. The dog will copy your movement and so develop a 'quartering' pattern that you can later control by arm signals if necessary. When this is tried for the first time try to find ground that is free of rabbits or other interesting forms of life. A rabbit or hare getting up in front of a youngster is always a great temptation and an even greater test of your obedience training. If your dog does start to chase all the earlier training is undone in a matter of a few seconds. The best help you can get is the use of a rabbit pen and it is not difficult to make one of these yourself if you have the ground. All you need is a small area with ground cover fenced in with small mesh wire. The wire needs to be buried at the sides to about eighteen inches to dissuade the rabbits from burrowing underneath. Alternatively, sheets of corrugated iron can be let into the ground along the sides to serve the same purpose. Once this pen is properly set up you can put in your rabbits. Take your dog into the pen on a long cord and encourage it to hunt. Once a rabbit is disturbed and runs into the open the dog must be checked on the

Hartshorn Ruby showing the rake of shoulder which is an operational necessity and which some show dogs do not have. The raised forepaw was her invariable habit when working, although she never did it with dummies.

cord to stop it chasing and a very definite command 'sit' given at the same time. After a time you will be able to take the dog into the run without a lead and rely on verbal commands and the whistle. If the lesson is forgotten and your dog gives chase there must be a quick command or whistle to 'sit' and then you must start over again using the check-cord. I have mentioned that your rabbit run should include natural cover so that the dog has to hunt to flush the rabbits but it is equally important that the rabbits should have an escape route from a determined and headstrong dog. Training is no easy task and for those of us who are really amateurs at the job it needs to be taken very seriously and slowly making sure that each lesoson is properly learned before progressing to the next stage. All your attention should be directed towards your dog's behaviour and I would suggest that at this stage you cannot take a gun and enjoy the shooting as well as control the dog. This is where you have to make a choice. Once I had trained my dogs to what I felt was a reasonable standard I sought invitations and opportunities to work behind the guns looking for the odd wounded bird or picking up for a syndicate that was short of Spaniel support. A word of caution however, some members of some syndicates have some very badly trained and ill-disciplined dogs which they feel their membership of the syndicate entitles them to bring along. Your own youngster can very soon learn some bad habits. If your dog behaves itself and does a good job it will not be difficult to obtain future invitations. In Chapter 7, when I was discussing hereditary faults and mouths in particular, I mentioned the hard-mouthed dog and all retrieving dogs must have a soft grip that does not crush. When you first get your dog retrieving shot game check it very carefully when it is brought back to you to ensure that the ribs have not been crushed. If this happens in competition your dog will be rejected and if it happens regularly you are wasting time and money in entry fees.

At some stage your dog may be required to retrieve from water and as a trial dog it will have to complete a water test. Most Springers like water and it is not difficult to get them to enter, but I have had one or two that needed very gentle persuasion and coaxing before they became really enthusiastic. It is as well to take your dog to a small and shallow stream where he can paddle and wade and so get used to the feel of water. He can even do a little retrieving in such a stream. You can gradually increase the distance of the retrieve and the depth of water until your dog feels confident. Extend this still further by teaching him to jump from the bank instead of seeking a shallow shelving entry point. Some of my dogs have to be very firmly kept out of water whilst another will go in but is not really interested.

Out on a shoot there will be other natural and man-made obstacles such as fences and so a youngster needs to be taught to jump. Of course they are natural jumpers as you may have noticed when you make a kennel run and the wire is not quite high enough. I train mine to jump in and out of small wire pens to retrieve dummies. Start with something quite small to give the dog confidence and gradually increase the height. As the height increases I favour something of the strength of sheep or pig wire as this appears to give the dog more confidence than a sloppy slack wire. I must admit that I have been a little distressed at times to see dogs sent over, or even being expected to retrieve over, several strands of taut barbed wire. I have seen some very deep and long cuts in a dog's abdomen resulting from this, which I felt was quite unnecessary merely to prove a point. I have noticed that the handlers have placed a jacket over the barbs before venturing over them themselves.

Earlier in this chapter I mentioned Mr Arkwright's quality of 'courage' and of course this is part of that willingness to face cover or any other form of obstacle in the quest to please. This brings me back to the question of cover and thorn bush. If a bird or rabbit is hidden away inside dense thorn, a good dog will do its best to push it out and it must be willing to do this. With more experience it may well push its head only into breaks in the thicket and achieve the same objective. Once you know your dog you will come to accept the situation if he moves on to another bush. A good dog will not waste time poking around and inside cover for no purpose. On the other hand if the thicket does hide the quarry then the dog must go in to get it out.

It may be that this is the stage where a great many people will be content with what they have achieved and will gain sufficient satisfaction from shooting with and working their own dog over rented ground or at the invitation of those operating syndicates. On the other hand you may wish to enter for competition at Field Trials. It would appear that the number so wishing is on the increase and there are indications that many dogs of low standard are being entered before they are really ready. This is most annoying to those who own properly trained and qualified dogs. This may sound rather strange and so I must explain the system of entering for Trials. Most Field Trial Societies and Clubs that organise qualifying Trials offer novice and open stakes. With entry in each limited to sixteen dogs it is obvious that many will be disappointed. Added to this the fact that members of the sponsoring bodies are usually given preference and the situation becomes even more difficult. Would be competitors join as many of the sponsoring bodies as possible in order to gain preference when all the entries are put in the hat and the first sixteen drawn make up the Stake. After that there is the reserve list for the stake but apart from illness or a bitch coming into season there is little chance of moving up into the runners.

In these novice stakes the draw can result in any member getting a run and on the surface this would appear to be quite fair. However, I am told that in many cases the standard of work has been poor and on more than one occasion the first prize has been withheld by the judges. I know of at least one well known trialer with winning stock who failed to get a nomination in a Novice Stake for a complete season. The Open Stake is rather different because any nomination is subject to a qualification based on previous wins but although the standard of work is assured there is still the problem of oversubscribed Stakes. The show people do not suffer from this problem as a class and entry can be any size subject to the judge's physical ability to cope with it in the time allowed and this is generally accepted as two hundred dogs per day in any breed classes. At sanction shows a variety puppy class may have as many as forty exhibits. Some societies who aim especially to help newcomers offer stakes for novice and amateur handlers. Here there is a qualification for both, firstly that the handler must not have previously won a prize handling at trials, and for the amateur handler he must not have trained or handled dogs for gain. This does offer the chance of a run against people of equal standing and experience. In the novice stake the only restriction is that the dog only is regarded as a beginner.

When writing about shows I suggested that a good way to gain knowledge of a breed was to act as a ring steward with a good judge. In much the same way it is very helpful to be able to act as steward for a field trial judge or even to be the number carrier. Both are right up in the line and there is a good view of the dogs and their handlers. Perhaps I should explain that the number carrier is the person, allocated one per judge, who holds up a frame containing a large card that indicates the number of the dog running at that moment under that particular judge.

What of the ordinary spectator? They are allowed, in fact they are welcomed but in attending they must place themselves under the control of the trial organisers. In effect this means that they are required to walk behind the red flag together with the competitors not actually running under the judges. The red flag carrier is just another little job that has to be done to ensure the safety of everyone. Spectators all over the place are a menace to themselves and everybody else.

The standard to be achieved requires a great deal of time, patience, experience and knowledge. I have only had the opportunity to glean a little from a few of the great men and although my life has been spent mainly with show blood lines I took to the working side, albeit in a simple and non-competitive way, simply because I realised the importance of the working instinct in the breed and at the same time for the added pleasure it gave me. I am sure that my dogs also gained some benefit.

I would not change my particular line of Springers for I have developed a strain as near as possible to what I want. There has been nothing commercial or competitive about it and the pleasure has come from possession of a few good looking dogs that could do a day's work in keeping with their ancestry.

There are a number of good books to be read about training methods. Some are old but so very helpful. Others are by contemporary Springer people who have spent a life time in the business.

10   Springers Abroad

The British have always had that little something that has enabled them to breed some of the finest livestock. Our horses and cattle have been greatly sought after and have left these shores to become foundation stock all over the world. Our dogs are no exception and I understand that the first export of an English Springer was to the United States in 1907 when two crossed the Atlantic to enter the kennel of Mr Robert Dumont in New Jersey. These, of course, were the first of many.

Our stock once it is abroad is usually competing under show and field trial regulations that are quite different from those laid down by our own Kennel Club. The National Kennel Clubs in each country are, as in Britain, the final authority within the national boundaries. They make the rules and regulations and see that they are enforced. There is, however, one important body which has considerable influence throughout the world and that is the Fereration Cynologique Internationale—generally referred to by the initials F.C.I. In very broad terms it is a federation of numerous national ruling authorities on canine affairs and its importance lies in the fact that it is able to award a title.

Individual countries, through their own Kennel Clubs, award the title of champion in a variety of ways but when awarded the dog so honoured is correctly *only a champion in its own country*. The F.C.I. has its own certificate known as the C.A.C.I.B. which, under certain circumstances, it will allow its member National Kennel Clubs to award at certain shows. The award of such a certificate will help a winning dog towards the title of International Champion. The F.C.I. is most definite that the only true International Champions are those that have qualified under its own rules and regulations. I have seen a number of pedigrees prepared in this country showing certain dogs as of International Champion status and this, of course, would not be accepted by F.C.I. The ruling of that body has no force in this country, however, as our own Kennel Club is not a member club but there is discussion from time to time on any particular urgent matter that may arise. In all fairness I believe it true to say that the F.C.I. has always been helpful in making sure that any breed standard adopted is the breed standard of the country from which the dog originated. It is, of course, the interpretation of the standards that causes the problems and again the F.C.I. has always been in favour of closer co-operation between the various national canine bodies. There is some opinion that our own Kennel Club could have gone further to forge closer links with the F.C.I.

There are a number of anomalies where closer co-operation would be helpful. For instance only in France and Italy is a dog running in a trial required to keep quiet. In other European countries they are expected to give tongue. Under our Kennel Club Rules this would lead to disqualification. A very obvious problem arises when we export trained dogs to these countries. As far as the Spaniel world is concerned some attempt has been made to air a few problems at the European Spaniel Congress which is held every third year in a country decided upon at the previous Congress. In Britain the late Dr Esther Rickards gave much time and energy to the business of forming the United Spaniel Association which most Spaniel Clubs joined in its earlier years. Although the Kennel Club gave its approval for the formation of the Association it is not a registered body and, therefore, lacks that little bit of authority that would make all the difference. Dr Rickards was, of course, extremely knowledgeable and a very strong personality and when she died some two years ago the Association found itself without a Secretary and it is still endeavouring to find somebody who could carry on this difficult role. For a very short time Mrs Kay Baldwin, then my husband and now Mrs Mavis Lancaster have been trying to keep the Association afloat. I am afraid that there are indications that the Association may go aground for much of the initial interest and will to co-operate has waned. It would appear that the dominance of the Cocker Spaniel Council and its member clubs has erected an obstacle as far as the other Spaniel breeds are concerned. Congress is always held in conjunction with a continental show and I well remember attending a particular Congress as a delegate for English Springers and a considerable part of the day had been taken up by the Cocker delegates discussing the trimming of the show coat, the method of plucking out dead head and expressing considerable abhorrence that clippers and scissors should ever be used, except, of course, where it is generally agreed that they need to be used. This was the day prior to the show and back at the hotel in the evening there was the usual activity by Congress members preparing their dogs for the following day. Our accommodation was somewhat square in shape with a central quadrangle which was used for parking some of the cars containing the dogs. During the course of the evening I looked out of the window and watched the preparation of the dogs and all the scissors were clipping away happily! I have mentioned this constant use of scissors and clippers earlier in the book because we must impress upon exhibitors that the method simply ruins coats. Of course the same thing is going on in this country all the time but I mention it out of interest to illustrate just how much time can be wasted just talking. Remember also that all the British Delegates were paying their expenses in full without any support from their Breed Clubs most of which were not strong enough financially to help in any case.

It may now be as well to give some information regarding the export of dogs. You will need an Export Pedigree and this is obtained on application to the Kennel Club and the current cost is £10. Regulations relating to the entry of livestock into different countries do vary and are obviously amended from time to time. Make sure that you have the latest and most up to date information available. You need to know what inoculations must be given and what certificates are required from your veterinary surgeon. A telephone call to the office of the Ministry of Fisheries and Agriculture (Small Animals Division) at Surbiton in Surrey, or even to the nearest Embassy or Consulate of the country concerned, will give you the information you require. Incorrect procedure will cause delays and possibly extra expense and in the meantime your dog may be held up in uncomfortable conditions whilst the paper work is being sorted out.

The United States

The English Springer has become very popular in the States where the first registration of the breed by the American Kennel Club was made in 1910, and in common with other Spaniels has been used with the gun.

The first show was held at Madison Square Gardens in New York in 1923 followed in 1924 by the formation of the English Springer Spaniel Field Trial Society which body issued a standard of points for the breed and rules for field trials. The first field trial was held in the same year and the winners at both shows and field trial were imports from England.

As in this country there is a distinct difference between the working and the show dog. This is hardly surprising when it is remembered that the foundation stock for both sides was imported and elsewhere I have mentioned F.T. Ch. Wakes Wager, F.T. Ch. Dalshangan Dandy Boy and F.T. Ch. Tedwyns Trex as trial exports. On the show side there were dogs like Ch. Showman of Shotton, Ch. Nuthill Dignity and Ch. Jambok of Ware to influence the breed. Unfortunately, I feel that the Americans have now exaggerated the show dog to such an extent that the type difference is even more marked than in this country.

A dog can qualify as a field trial champion if it wins two all-aged stakes in which at least ten dogs are entered. The water test is compulsory before qualification. Although two judges are appointed for

the trial and they take 'odds' and 'evens' as over here they do not change over and it is only in the run-off that the judge sees the dogs unseen by him in the first walk through. However, strange as it may seem to us, no dog can receive an award unless it has run under both judges.

There are general championship shows where classes for English Springers are scheduled and then specialist breed shows. The American Kennel Club lays down the rules and the classification is somewhat differently arranged. However, a group system of judging is used and so the judge arrives at a Best in Show award in a manner similar to our own. The title of Champion is not the result of the award of three challenge certificates but on a total of points awarded from show to show, the maximum obtainable at any one show being five. The points are allocated according to the size of the entry and no dog can become a champion in less than three shows. The system sounds as if it could be the alternative to the 'cheap certificates' we hear mentioned in this country. However, a good American entry giving the maximum points could well be made up of poor quality exhibits and I

Am. Ch. Melilotus Shooting Star owned by the late Mrs Mary Scott and imported by her from Mrs H. Gilman Smith.

have been told that this happens. America's most famous show dog has been Frejax Royal Salute for he created an unbeaten record in the number of times that he won the Sporting Group and Best in Show at championship shows.

In my early days as Secretary of our English Springer Spaniel Club I had considerable correspondence with Mrs Gasow whose Ch. Sir Lancelot of Salilyn was the sire of Royal Salute and also Colonel J. C. Quirk, who owned the winning Greenfair show and trial kennels. Mrs H. Gilman Smith has made up many champions and elsewhere I have mentioned her export to England for Mrs Mary Scott as a possible outcross to Boxer of Bramhope.

Canada

The Springer is equally as popular in Canada as in the States. Mr R. Chevrier was an early importer of the breed and it was to him that Dual Ch. Flint of Avendale was sent. A great deal of the initial influence came from a number of imported dogs carrying the *Beechgrove* prefix and several were sent across in the period immediately after the end of the First World War. It has been suggested that the dog that had the greatest influence on Springers was Ch. Don Juan of Gerwyn imported in 1914. This dog was black and white and sired by Corrin of Gerwyn a red and white dog whose name is to be found in many old pedigrees of Welsh Springers.

The Standard for the Breed is the same as in the United States but there is a separate Canadian Kennel Club. Show and Field Trial Regulations are not the same.

Kenya

Control of 'dogdom' is in the hands of the East African Kennel Club and two general championship shows are held each year. At the present time Springers are not well represented but a number of years ago I knew Mrs Spencer Tryon quite well and she was a great supporter of the breed. As in England a dog needs three Challenge Certificates to become a champion. I have had the privilege of having judged twice in Kenya during the last ten years and have always been disappointed at the absence of good Springers. I understand that no official Spaniel Trials have been organised since the end of the Second World War. The political situation over the past few years has not been easy and at the same time I am not too sure that a heavily coated dog such as a Springer is really suited to the climate.

Zimbabwe and South Africa

I have little up to date information on canine affairs since the political restructuring of this part of Africa. Originally the controlling body was the Rhodesian Federation Kennel Club which was affiliated to the South Africa Kennel Union. Rhodesians did, however, have their own title Champion (Rho.) which was obtained by winning four challenge certificates under four different judges in the two Rhodesias as they then existed. These certificates could be counted towards a South African title. Of course, distances were very great and Mr and Mrs Foden wrote me long letters describing their routes of travel in making up Ch. (Rho.) Kim of Renfrew and Ch. (Rho.) Jancy of Stubham imported as a puppy from Mrs Kay Till of the Stubham Kennels.

During the Second World War Princess Radziwill, in exile from her home in Poland, lived in England and took up an interest in Springers having bought *Whaddon Chase* stock from Lady Lambe. She established her own prefix, *Ira*, and after the war went to live in South Africa where she helped to establish the breed. Bob of Ira, owned by Mr and Mrs Raesides, later became a Champion (Rho.). The *Renfrew* prefix of Mrs L. R. Penny was well known in South Africa and two of her imports Studley Hussar and Diamond of Stubham were made up and later added Ch. (Rho.) when she moved to Rhodesia. An import from Mr E. A. Anderson, Candyfloss of Crosslane had considerable influence on the breed through the litters bred from her whilst she herself won five challenge certificates and two reserves. As in Zimbabwe, South Africa now appears to be lacking in Springers both in quantity and quality.

Australia

Each State has its own separate authority for the administration of shows and trials. Throughout all the States the points system is operated and to gain the title of champion a dog must have 100 points and four challenge certificates under four different judges. The title of field trial champion can be obtained by competing in classes for 'Spaniels and Retrievers' but the game laws vary in some States and there is difficulty with working Springers. Field Trials are, however, very popular in Victoria, and are run on rabbits and quail. The chief strains established in Victoria and other parts of Australia were related to the early imports around 1930 of *Beauchief*, *Ranscombe* and *Cairnies* stock. Some of these carried blood lines that could be traced back to the *Aqualate* lines. Whilst Dual Champions in this country have been limited to three, Australia produced two early on and these were Aust. Dual Ch. Curtsey Chicquita and Aust. Dual Ch. Curtsey George. They were progeny of Whittlemoor Flicker imported into Australia by Dr M. Wilson in 1947 from Mr A. E. Curtis. Later 'George' was to come to England and spend the rest of his life with Miss Morland Hooper. There was also some *Winch* blood in Victoria for in 1950 Mrs G. G. Crawford exported Winch Pyrites. This strain always produced

Sh. Ch. Moorcliff
Freetwood
Gamecock owned in
the U.K. by Mr
Ernest Froggatt and
exported to
Australia.

quality stock. Pyrites became an Australian Champion and her descendants produced eight more in later years.

For many years Mrs Helen Sapio owned the most Springers in Queensland although she had previously lived in New Zealand. Her best known Australian dogs were Ch. Puni Maiden of Cruchfield, Ch. Cruchfield Puni Luia and Cruchfield Kiwa. At the present time, the breed enjoys considerable popularity and many present day winners are related to fairly recent imports from *Moorcliff, Hawkhill* and *Clevehill* stock.

New Zealand
The controlling body for shows is the New Zealand Kennel Club and for field trials the Dominion Gundog Club. Springers have been popular in New Zealand, particularly as shooting dogs, for there is always rabbit shooting available and duck and quail can be shot in winter. As elsewhere, the Springer has shown his ability as an all round gun dog. Just before the beginning of the Second World War, two dogs, F.T. Ch. Welford Trump and Anthony of Somersby, were imported from England and their progeny have formed the foundation of many working and show kennels in the country and their names will be found in a number of older pedigrees. The outstanding dogs at this time were F.T. Ch. Three Star, F.T. Ch. Chum and Ch. Sandhurst

Solitaire. The latter dog won his title on the bench, many placings at trials and it was only the beginning of the war, when all trials were cancelled, that robbed him of his field title. Two other imports, Slice O'Vara and Strike O'Vara made a marked impression at trials and many wins can be credited to their progeny. A daughter of Strike, owned by Mr J. Stanton of the *Dalkey* kennel, had the distinction of being the only Springer to win the New Zealand All Breeds Championship—her name was F.T. Ch. Dalkey Dabble. Notable show Springers in the two Islands have been Ch. Sandhurst Salute, Ch. Sandhurst Sherman, Ch. Patricia of Worthy Down and Ch. Brackenfield Broom. Salute and Sherman were also notable winners at trials. Mrs C. Cooper of Ashburton was really the outstanding personality in Springers for she was breeding and showing her dogs for many years and was the first woman to train and handle Springers at trials.

A short time ago I met Mrs Evans who used to live near us at Stroud in Gloucestershire. She went to live in New Zealand some years ago and was back in England for a short holiday combined with a general look around for good stock to take back. Her own breed is the Golden Retriever but she spoke well of the working Springers in her new homeland.

Switzerland

The administration of all canine affairs is carried out by the Schweizerische Kynologische Gesellschaft. In an early visit to Switzerland I was taken to see Frau. Richei who had imported a dog from the *Colmaris* kennel of Mr Sandy Davies. She was showing Springers in the middle 1960s. In 1957 the Swiss Kennel Club recognised the formation of an English Springer Spaniel Club but some years later it joined with the Retrievers to form a combined club. The President is Frau. Leonie Bernhauser of Rapperswil whom I have known for many years. She imported some of my stock and made Larkstoke Wagwing into a Swiss champion. At the present time Mr Grimauld, Mrs K. Hubacher and Mr U. Hitzig (Geneva) are breeding winning stock. I have judged several times in Switzerland and still find the system somewhat difficult.

France

The controlling body is the French Kennel Club but there is also a French Spaniel Club which is very influential. I have judged different breeds in France on a number of occasions and whilst I do not really like the system of judging, the French regulations regarding title qualifications do appeal to me. To become a bench champion, a dog must win its three certificates under different judges and must also obtain a commendation at a field trial. Likewise the working dog in

Int. Ch. Larkstoke
Nuthatch bred by
the author and sold
to M. Thorp of
Paris.

addition to its awards in the field must obtain a place and qualification
at a show. In a field event, there must be at least six runners in a stake
for a win to count towards the title. It is good to know that there is this
insistence on the combination of work and looks. The French Spaniel
Club has a very dynamic President in the person of M. Gilbert Thorp
who has done so much to support the breed. Some years ago now he
bought a youngster from me at Crufts and in France this was to
become Int. Ch. Larkstoke Nuthatch winning both on the bench and at
trials.

After the Second World War a number of dogs were imported from
England carrying blood lines of the Brandyhole (originating from
Stubham), Bramhope, Stokeley, Higham and Woodbay kennels.
Current winning stock is in the hands of French Members of the
English Club including Mlle. Chavernac and Dr LeBrun.

Italy

The Italian Kennel Club is the controlling body but a Spaniel Club was formed in 1958. There are shows and field trials which are run on a system very similar to our own. As in France, the show and trial dog must gain a qualification in each activity before the title can be awarded. Some of the earlier imports were made by Signor Marco Valcarenghi from the *Stokeley* and *Higham* kennels and these formed the foundation for Mr Valcarenghi's own *Valmarco* kennel which has been very successful on the bench and at trials. The Springer has become quite popular with a number of shooting people.

Holland

The Dutch Kennel Club is the ruling body but there is a Dutch Spaniel Club. Springers are not numerous and of imports from England the first to gain its title was Dutch Ch. Winch Crocidolite. I was, of course, very pleased to send out a bitch, later to become Dutch Ch. Larkstoke Sarcelle, that took top awards in breed classes including a Best in Show award at Utrecht in 1972 when some 1,500 dogs of all breeds were exhibited. To become Champion in Holland, a dog must have won four championship prizes at four differnt shows but if one of these happens to be the Winners Show at Amsterdam then only three are required. A field trial champion must win two field trial championship prizes and obtain a qualification at a show. Judging in Holland recently I was not too happy with the quality of many present day exhibits.

Sweden

The Swedish Kennel Club is the controlling body for shows and field trials. Springers have a good classification at most Shows and in the main are the progeny of imported stock from America and England. English blood lines sent out came from the *Whaddon Chase, Higham, Woodbay, Stubham* and *Larkstoke* kennels. After the Second World War two well known importers, breeders and exhibitors were the Baroness Hermelin and Mrs Sigrun Wallgvrist. In current times the winning stock is mostly related to the *Hawkhill* and *Cleavehill* blood lines. Full champions must qualify on bench and in the field.

Springers have, of course, been exported to many other parts of the world but I have restricted my comments to those countries where the breed might be regarded as reasonably well established. The making of an Int. Champion is not that difficult in Europe for with no quarantine regulations to restrict movement dogs can be taken to the International Shows and so gain the qualification subject to the passing of the appropriate tests. We should also remember that competition is not so high as in this country where you may now encounter up to thirty exhibits in any one class.

I think it important that we should strive, through whatever machinery may be available, to maintain the standards that we have laid down for our native breeds. There is the danger of mis-interpretation leading to unwelcome change. To some extent this danger exists here—the idea of changing a Standard to fit a dog rather than changing the dog to fit the Standard

11   Clubs and Societies

The Kennel Club is the ruling body of 'dogdom' and, like any other similar body, comes in for a considerable degree of criticism. Elsewhere in this book I have mentioned the tremendous increase in the number of shows and the difficulty in being able to secure a nomination for the field trials. As all these events are held under Kennel Club Rules and Regulations the participating dogs must be registered and so it is easy to see that the work of the Registrations Department at least will have developed to such an extent that the normal method of working can no longer keep pace with the work. Readers who have been following developments through the canine press will know that there is talk of computerisation etc. in an effort to clear the backlog of work and make for a more effective and efficient system for future years. In the meantime, breeders are experiencing delays with registrations and other details.

In many ways so similar to the Jockey Club, the Kennel Club is self-perpetuating in that membership is limited in numbers and election is subject to nomination by existing members and approval by the appropriate Committee. Until the present time membership has been restricted to men although for many years there has been a Ladies' Branch based in the same building. The Ladies' Branch also had a limited membership and election was based on the same principle as for the men. Over the past two or three years women in 'dogdom' have been making efforts to secure a place in the direct management of canine affairs and as I put together material for this book, a decision has been taken to allow women the privilege of full membership of the Kennel Club with seats on the various Committees. The Ladies' Branch has ceased to exist and only time will tell just how many of its members will finally seek and obtain election to the Kennel Club as full members. In the show world, of course, the number of women involved is far in excess of the number of men but it remains to be seen what difference their inclusion on Kennel Club Committees will make as the problems of co-ordinating and organising shows and field trials will remain the same no matter who sits on the Committees. We can only hope that those elected to the Committees are those who are directly involved with these events and are fully aware of all the problems.

Useful publications—Regulations, Lists of Breed Societies etc. are:
Annual—*Kennel Club Year Book*
Annual—*Kennel Club Stud Book*
Monthly—*Kennel Club Gazette*
All communications to the ruling body should be addressed as follows:

The Secretary,
The Kennel Club,
1 Clarges Street,
Piccadilly,
London, W1Y 8AB

The oldest existing body covering all Spaniel breeds is the Spaniel Club which was founded in 1885. This Club drew up Standards of Points for the Spaniel breeds in an effort to guide breeders along what was considered to be the right lines. At this early stage of the development of all the Spaniels, differences of opinion began to arise between those whose interest centred on show activities and those who were mainly concerned with work in the field. The Club had an idea that the best way to counteract any of these differences would be to hold field trials but did nothing about it until January 1900, when a Trial was held at Welbeck Abbey with Mr C. A. Phillips (co-author of *The Sporting Spaniel*) and Mr James Farrow as judges. However, the very idea of Trials led to the formation of another body, The Sporting Spaniel Society, which held a trial in January 1899 at Sutton Scarsdale when Mr Elias Bishop and Mr William Arkwright (author of *The Pointer and His Predecessors 1902*) were the judges. The Society held a further trial in December of the same year. However, after being a little slow at the start, the Spaniel Club survived and right up to the present time has maintained its interest in and support for the field trial movement. Its membership has never been large but has always included most of the well known field trialers. In recent years the Club has taken over the running of the Spaniel Championship for the Kennel Club and this would appear a fitting arrangement for the Senior Spaniel Club. The name and address of the current Secretary is:

Mr C. Sutcliffe
Maguga,
Woodcock Heath,
Kingstone,
Uttoxeter,
Staffs, ST14 8QS.

This brings me to the Clubs and Societies which exist exclusively for the benefit of the English Springer Spaniel. The English Springer Spaniel Club is the Senior Club having been founded in 1921 at a meeting held after Cruft's Show. Having recently retired as Secretary to the Club, a position I held for some twenty-five years, I would not wish to comment on the activities of the Clubs as a whole. All the others are regional bodies and each is doing a great deal to support the breed and to provide the facilities demanded by its membership. Most provide show facilities and the majority organise trials and I will list them accordingly:

Clubs/Societies Holding Shows and Field Trials

The English Springer Spaniel Club:
Secretary: Mrs Carolyn Muirhead,
'Shipden',
Long Lane,
Colby,
Norwich,
Norfolk.

The English Springer Spaniel Club of Wales:
Secretary: Mrs E. Green,
45, Heol Tawe,
Abercrave,
Swansea,
S. Wales.

The English Springer Spaniel Club of Scotland:
Secretary: Mrs E. K. Thompson,
Rivington Lodge,
Castle Douglas,
Kirkcudbrightshire

The Midland English Springer Spaniel Society:
Secretary: Mrs J. Backhouse,
121, Silcoates Lane,
Wrenthorpe,
Wakefield,
Yorks

Clubs/Societies Holding Shows

The Southern English Springer Spaniel Society:
Mr D. Miller,
Beacon View Kennels,
St Leonards Road,
Chivery,
Nr. Tring, Herts.

The Northern English Springer Spaniel Society:
Mrs E. Dobson,
Teesview Kennels,
Neasham,
Darlington,
Co. Durham.

Clubs/Societies Holding Field Trials

The English Springer Spaniel Club of N. Ireland:
Mr R. E. Clemitson,
Fairacres,
1, Holywood Road,
Newtownards,
Co. Down, N.I.

The Antrim & Down Springer Spaniel Club:
Mr R. B. McLean,
13, Mandeville Avenue,
Lisburn,
Co. Antrim, N.I.

There are also a number of General Field Trial Societies organising Field Trials for Spaniels and the Stakes they offer are usually 'any variety' which means that English Springers are eligible. In point of fact the English Springer has little competition except from the Cocker Spaniel and the occasional Welsh Springer. A list of these General Field Trial Societies is in the *Kennel Club Year Book*.

If you want to keep up-to-date with show results and general comment on the dog world it will be useful to take one or both of the weekly dog papers, *Dog World* and *Our Dogs*. For general commment and results of field trials I have found *Shooting Times* very useful and on the broader front to include hunting items etc. then of course *The Field*. All are obtainable through your local newsagent.

Appendix 1

Registration Table for English Springers from 1919

1919	29	*1943*	779
1920	156	*1944*	1326
1921	394	*1945*	2035
1922	690	*1946*	3250
1923	1122	*1947*	3172
1924	1208	*1948*	2740
1925	1432	*1949*	2327
1926	1256	*1950*	2316
1927	1328	*1951*	1669
1928	1271	*1952*	1458
1929	1229	*1953*	1398
1930	1104	*1954*	1376
1931	1017	*1955*	1341
1932	942	*1956*	1328
1933	927	*1957*	1305
1934	996	*1958*	1477
1935	1075	*1959*	1535
1936	1085	*1960*	1613
1937	1066	*1961*	1616
1938	1149	*1962*	1941
1939	608	*1963*	1944
1940	207	*1964*	1832
1941	182	*1965*	2004
1942	386	*1966*	1796

1967	2054
1968	2147
1969	2524
1970	2529
1971	2683
1972	3658
1973	3781
1974	4333
1975	4472
1976	2061
1977	1357

N.B. The marked drop in registrations for the years 1976 and 1977 does not indicate a decrease in breed popularity but is the result of the problems in the Registrations Department at the Kennel Club resulting in the non-processing of so many applications. No figures are yet available for 1978 and 1979.

Appendix 2

Post-World War II Champions

Name	Sex	Breeder	Owner
Whaddon Chase Snipe	B	Mr T. Hill	Lady Lambe
Whaddon Chase Bonny Tom	D	Mr T. Hill	Lady Lambe
Solitaire of Happeedaze	D	Mr S. Phipp	Mr W. R. Hepplewhite
Stokeley Bonny Boy	D	Mr D. C. Hannah	Mr D. C. Hannah
Invader of Ide	D	Mr T. Richie	Mr J. H. J. Braddon
Sandylands Shrubley	D	Mr M. D. Withers	Mrs G. Broadley
Sandylands Soubranie	D	Mrs G. Broadley	Mr E. Lumb Taylor
Sprightley of Happeedaze	B	Mr E. N. Power	Mr W. R. Hepplewhite
Stokeley Bonny Boy	D	Mr D. C. Hannah	Mr D. C. Hannah
Staitley May Queen	B	Mr F. Taggart	Mr G. Harwell
Higham Topsy	B	Lady Lambe	Miss C. M. Francis
Carnfield Chick	B	Mr G. A. Taylor	Mr G. A. Taylor
Carnfield Florrie	B	Mr D. C. Hannah	Mr G. A. Taylor
Light of Ashleigh	B	Mr F. L. Davey	Mr A. B. Nicholson
Castlecary Cameronian	D	Mr F. Chalmers	Mrs G. Broadley
Jess of Montcrief	B	Mr E. W. Dugeon	Mr E. W. Dugeon
Carnfield Albvic Legioner	D	Mr A. V. Blake	Mr G. A. Taylor
Whaddon Chase Prince	D	Lady Lambe	Lady Lambe
Sandylands Shandy	D	Mrs G. Broadley	Mrs G. Broadley
Strathblane Bonnie	D	Major A. M. Horsbrugh	Mr S. O'Flynn
Leymor Recorder	D	Mr R. A. Morgan	Mr R. A. Morgan
Birkdale Beggermaid	B	Mr W. Manin	Mrs N. Ireland
Stokeley Gay Boy	D	Mr D. C. Hannah	Mr D. C. Hannah
Banner of Beechfield	D	Mrs F. Thompson	Miss J. Wilkins
Stokeley Lucky	D	Mr D. C. Hannah	Mr D. C. Hannah
Alexander of Stubham	D	Mrs F. O. Till	Mrs F. O. Till
Bramhope Recorder	D	Mr & Mrs J. Scott	Mr E. Froggatt
Whaddon Chase Bracken	B	Lady Lambe	Lady Lambe
Peter of Lortonfell	D	Mr F. L. Davey	Mr J. C. Hanning
Clintonhouse George	D	Mrs G. Thomson	Mr I. Davies
Whaddon Chase Bonny Lass	B	Lady Lambe	Lady Lambe
Tillan Toddy	B	Lady Belhaven	Mr J. M. Bolton
Colmaris Contessa	B	Mr I. Davies	Mr I. Davies
Dinah of Stubham	B	Mrs F. O. Till	Mr R. Grant
Studley Major	D	Mrs S. G. Smithson	Mrs S. G. Smithson
Belarosa of Bramhope	B	Mr A. Laing	Mr & Mrs J. Scott
Camdin Chief	D	Mrs V. Hare-Dinsley	Mrs V. Hare-Dinsley
Beanmore Camdin Greta	B	Mrs V. Hare-Dinsley	Mrs H. P. Frankish

Print of Ardrick	D Mr F. G. Burton	Mr F. G. Burton
Bonnie Wee Teal	B Mr A. R. Webster	Mr J. S. Webster
Inverruel Raider	D Mr T. Robb	Mr D. Campbell
Whaddon Chase Grouse	B Lady Lambe	Lady Lambe
Northdown Donna	B Mr W. Manin	Mrs F. Sherwood & Mr W. Manin
Duchess of Stubham	B Mrs F. O. Till	Mrs J. Spence
Mowgrain Mr Chips	D Mrs J. Midgeley	Mrs J. Midgeley
Bathsheba of Bramhope	B Mr & Mrs J. Scott	Mrs M. Scott
Royal Salute of Stubham	D Mrs F. O. Till	Mrs F. O. Till
Studley Diadem	B Mrs S. G. Smithson	Mrs F. O. Till
Colmaris Chancellor	D Mr I. Davies	Mrs H. P. Frankish
Hawkhill Brave	D Miss J. Robinson	Miss J. Robinson
Floravon Silverstar	B Mr H. Sweeney	Miss J. Robinson
Tyneview Margaret	B Mr G. Scott	Mrs E. Dobson
Winch Starturn	D Mrs G. G. Crawford	Mrs G. G. Crawford
Brandyhole Diadem	B Mrs J. Spence	Mrs J. Spence
Hyperion of Stubham	D Miss J. Robinson	Mrs F. O. Till
Sir Knight	D Mr J. Cranston	Mr J. Cranston
Glenford Gamester	D Mr H. F. Lock	Mr H. F. Lock
Beanmore George	D Mrs H. P. Frankish	Mrs H. P. Frankish
Maydown Ripple	B Mr H. Bunting	Mrs L. Bunting
Pencloe Driftwood	D Miss M. H. Bolton	Miss M. H. Bolton
Conneil Casket	B Mrs C. Crawford	Mr D. Storie
Pats Boy of Stodhart	D Mrs A. Campbell	Mr & Mrs T. P. and Mr N. P. Campbell
Stokeley Teesview Telstar	B Mrs E. Dobson	Mr D. C. Hannah
Moorcliff Dougal of Truelindale	D Miss M. Alder	Mr E. Froggatt
Blossomtime of Bramhope	B Mrs M. C. Scott	Mr & Mrs J. Backhouse
Chipmunk of Stubham	D Mrs F. O. Till	Mr F. J. Robinson
Woodbay Gay Charmer	B Mrs F. Sherwood	Mr N. H. Jenkins
Ranjoa Roberta	B Mr A. Lupton	Mr A. Lupton
Inverruel Pacemaker	D Mr D. Campbell	Mr D. Campbell
Larkstoke Ptarmigan	B Mrs I. B. Hampton	Mrs I. B. Hampton
Teesview Titus	D Mrs E. Dobson	Mrs E. Dobson
Weaversvale Moorcliff Farewell	B Mr E. Froggatt	Mr A. G. Nicholls
Teesview Tarmac	D Mrs E. Dobson	Mrs E. Dobson
Swallowtail of Shipden	D Mr P. Snowley	Mr & Mrs C. J. Muirhead
Pericles of Truelindale	D Miss M. Alder	Mr K. Hubbard
Sotherton Phantom of Shipden	D Mr & Mrs B. Smith	Mr & Mrs C. J. Muirhead
Berwin Suzette	B Mr J. Edwards	Mr P. Green
Larkstoke Grisette	B Mrs I. B. Hampton	Mrs I. B. Hampton
Cliffhill Julius	D Mrs T. D. Sheppard	Mrs T. D. Sheppard

Appendix 3

Post-World War II Field Trial Champions

Name	Sex Breeder	Owner
Spark O'Vara	D Mr Selwyn C. Jones	Mr Selwyn C. Jones
Silverstar of Chrishall	D Mr J. Kent	Mr J. Kent
Pinehawk Roger	D Mr A. Wylie	Mr A. Wylie
Sarkie O'Vara	D Mr Selwyn C. Jones	Mr Selwyn C. Jones
Caerleon Comet	D Mr T. Evans	Mr H. Thornel Brown
Whittlemoor George	D Mr A. E. Curtis	Col. C. McNeill
Racedale Rover	D Mr A. Wylie	Mrs A. Beale
Breckonhill Bee	B Mr T. H. Graham	Mr G. Curle
Spurt O'Vara	D Mr Selwyn C. Jones	Mr Selwyn C. Jones
Kinmount Pat	D Capt. E. W. Brook	Mr J. Buie
Acheron Pat	B Capt. A. McNeill Farquhar	Mr R. N. Burton
Rivington Glensaugh Glean	D Mr D. Munro	Messrs E. & M. Ainsworth
Whittlesford Record	D Col. C. McNeill	Col. C. McNeill
Acheron Trick	B Capt. A. McNeill Farquhar	Dr E. B. Sunderland
Sleet O'Vara	D Mr Selwyn C. Jones	Mr Selwyn C. Jones
Dauntless Monty	D Mr W. G. Sheldon	Mr W. G. Sheldon
Criffel Daisy Bell	B Mr T. B. Laird	Mr T. B. Laird
Greatford Kim	D Mr A. Sergeant	Major H. Peacock
Ludlow Gyp	B Mr W. G. Sheldon	Mr W. G. Sheldon
Criffel Pamela	B Mr T. B. Laird	Mr T. B. Laird
Stranwood Superior	D Mr J. McHarrie	Mr J. McHarrie
Carlo of Chrishall	D Mr P. R. A. Moxon	Mr J. Kent
Streonshalh Comet	B Mr R. Baker	Mr F. George
Ludlovian Darkie	D Mr W. G. Sheldon	Mr W. G. Sheldon
Staxigoe Sensation	B Mr J. Lindsay	Mr W. Emsleigh
Stranwood Speed	D Mr J. McHarrie	Mr J. McHarrie
Scramble O'Vara	B Mr Selwyn C. Jones	Mr Selwyn C. Jones
Ludlovian Ruby	B Mr W. G. Sheldon	Mr W. G. Sheldon
Saighton's Scent	B Mr T. Ratcliffe	Mr T. Ratcliffe
Carswell Cornelia	B Mrs P. M. Badenach Nicolson	Mrs P.M. Badenach Nicolson
Rivington Michele	B Mr W. G. Sheldon	Mrs C. A. Thomson
Criffel Nellie	B Mr T. B. Laird	Mr T. B. Laird
Cammas Tiny	B Mr G. Gibson	Mr J. M. Lukies
Ludlovian Bruce	D Mr W. G. Sheldon	Mr W. G. Sheldon
Criffel Prince	D Mr T. B. Laird	Mr T. B. Laird
Saighton's Sentry	D Mr Talbot Radcliffe	Mr Talbot Radcliffe
Gwen of Barnacre	B Mr Talbot Radcliffe	Mr H. Jackson
Criffel Danny	D Mr T. B. Laird	Mr T. B. Laird
Ludlovian Socks	D Mr W. G. Sheldon	Mrs F. E. Waller
Bryanston Bess	B Mr S. Folwell	Mr D. Bowlby

Rivington Landmark	D	Mr J. Windle	Mrs C. A. Thomson
Rossend Prince	D	Mr J. P. Winterbourne	Lt. Cmdr. E. A. J. Collard
Carswell Contessa	B	Mrs P.M. Badenach Nicolson	Mrs P. M. Badenach Nicolson
Breckonhill Brave	D	Mr G. Curle	Mr R. Garvin
Posterngate Jet	B	Mr C. Weighton	Dr D. A. White
Staxzigoe Seawaif	B	Mr D. McKenzie	Mr W. J. McCoubray
Rivington Raechele	B	Mrs C. A. Thomson	Mrs C. A. Thomson
Pinehawk Sark	D	Mr T. Evans	Mr A. Wylie
Breckonhill Bridegroom	D	Mr G. Curle	Mr G. Curle
Saighton's Spree	D	Mr H. Blackburn	Mr H. Blackburn
Richard of Elan	D	Mr A. Winterbourne	Lt. Cmdr. E. A. J. Collard
Jordieland Glean	D	Mr J. Windle	Mr J. Windle
Breckonhill Borderance Bounce	D	Mr D. S. Nicholson	Mr G. Curle
Entonlee Cherry	B	Mrs J. C. Lee	Mr F. George
Criffel Snipe	D	Mr T. B. Laird	Mr T. B. Laird
Harpersbrook Boots	D	Mr R. B. Weston-Webb	Mrs F. Goerge
Shineradee	D	Mr F. Bell	Mr F. George
Wakefares Sprigg	D	Mr F. M. Prime	Mr F. M. Prime
Pinehawk Spur	D	Mr T. Evans	Mr H. Silley
Willy of Barnacre	D	Mr H. Jackson	Mr H. Jackson
Jontis Jezebel	B	Mr K. Patterson	Mr R. J. Fettis
Blatherwycke Meadowcourt Hector	D	Mr R. B. Weston-Webb	Mrs F. George
Harpersbrook Reed	D	Mr H. Woodfield	Mr F. George
Red Siren	B	Mr W. Plunkett	Mr H. Thompson
Criffel Melody	B	Mr T. B. Laird	Mr T. B. Laird
Micklewood Slip	B	Mr F. Thomas	Capt. R. W. Corbett
Jonkit Jasper	D	Dr T. K. Davidson	Dr T. K. Davidson
Saighton's Swing	D	Mr Talbot Radcliffe	Mr Talbot Radcliffe
Speckle of Chrishall	B	Miss C. M. Francis	Mr J. Kent
Markdown Muffin	D	Mr F. Thomas	Mr F. Thomas
Dinas Dewi Sele	B	Mr Wm. Llewellyn	Major L. T. Spittle
Rivington Judy	B	Mr C. A. Thomson	Mr R. D. Methven
Meadowcourt Judy	B	Mr R. B. Weston-Webb	Mr R. B. Weston-Webb
Breckonhill Bilko	D	Mr W. C. Kyle	Mr G. Curle
Kate of Barnacre	B	Mr H. Jackson	Mr H. Jackson
Harpersbrook Reed	D	Mr H. A. Woodfield	Mr F. George
Jonkit Jandy	B	Dr T. K. Davidson	Mr B. B. Dutton
Markdown Mag	D	Mr J. B. Taylor	Mrs C. M. Thomas
Ballyvoy Dandy	D	Mr H. Thompson	Mr H. Thompson
Saighton's Shingle	B	Mr Talbot Radcliffe	Mrs R. Hadcock
Templegrafton Hardy	D	Mrs W. H. Whitbread	Capt. T. M. Lonsdale
Ruffin Tuff	D	Mr H. Johnston	Mr J. M. Kelvey
Gwibernant Abereithy Skip	D	Mr W. Llewellyn	Mr K. Erlandson
Gwibernant Gynan	D	Mr K. Erlandson	Mr R. J. Fettis
Wilby Trigger	D	Dr T. K. Davidson	Mr F. George
Criffel Patsy	B	Mr T. B. Laird	Mr T. B. Laird
Saighton's Stinger	D	Mr Talbot Radcliffe	Mr Talbot Radcliffe
Berrystead Freckle	B	Dr T. K. Davidson	Mr W. C. Williams
Gardez	B	Mr H. Johnston	Mr R. Garvan
Denhead Walnut	D	Mr D. M. Douglas	Mr G. S. Drummond

Willie Snaffles	D	Capt. W. Corbett	Mrs J. W. Sloan
Bradenham Socks	D	Mrs K. Luttmer	Mr K. Luttmer & Dr D. A. White
Meadowcourt Polly	B	Mr R. B. Weston-Webb	Mrs S. Weston-Webb
Lytchmore Hamers Jean	B	Mr B. B. Dutton	Mr M. H. Hopper
Wivenwood Fofo	B	Mr J. W. Davey	Mr J. W. Davey
Hiwood Rosso	D	Mr R. Haddow	The Hon. Lady Hill-Wood
Denhead Warrior	D	Mr D. M. Douglas	Mr D. M. Douglas
Blatherwycke Teal	D	Mr M. Jackson	Mrs F. George
Sliguy of Ardoon	D	Mr W. Sloan	Mr J. Magee
Saighton's Saulson	D	Mr Talbot Radcliffe	Mr Talbot Radcliffe
Meadowcourt Della	B	Mr R. B. Weston-Webb	Mr R. B. Weston-Webb
Hamers Hansel	D	Mr B. B. Dutton	Mr B. B. Dutton
Harwes Mitten	B	Mr E. E. Dougill	Mr D. Bovill
Jonkit Joel	D	Dr T. K. Davidson	Dr T. K. Davidson
Lytchmore Logan	D	Mr M. H. Hopper	Mr F. George
Wakefares Scamp	D	Mr H. Martineau	Mr F. M. Prime
Micklewood Story	B	Capt. R. W. Corbett	Capt. R. W. Corbett
Sallie of Barnacre	B	Mr R. Greenbank	Mr P. Jackson
Goldeneye Jock	D	Mr J. W. Gillett	Mr M. Greenwood
Joss of Barnacre	D	Mrs B. Jackson	Mr H. Jackson
Carswell Blanche	B	Mrs P. Badenach Nicolson	Mrs P. M. Badenach Nicolson
Markdown Marcus	D	Mr J. Sherlock	Mr F. Thomas
Bricksclose Scilla	B	Mrs M. Pratt	Mrs M. Pratt
Drumbro Daisy	B	Mr G. Eatson	Major G. Yool
Rivington Santa Claus	D	Mrs E. K. Thomson	Mrs E. K. Thomson
Gwibernant Garran	B	Lt. Col. L. T. Spittle	Lt. Col. L. T. Spittle
Lancshot Laser	D	Mr K. Erlandson	Mr C. C. Lamb
Braiswood Pimm	B	Mr J. W. Davey	Mrs E. M. Hartt
Lady of Ardoon	B	Mrs C. Spittle	Mr W. C. Sloan
Layerbrook Michelle	B	Mr M. Scales	Mr M. Scales
Harwes Silas	D	Dr D. Bovill	Dr D. Bovill
Berrystead Finch	D	Mr J. W. Davey	Mr W. C. Williams
Homerton Rock	B	Mr A. F. Ebbs	Mr A. F. Ebbs
Staxigoe Swank	D	Mr D. Mackenzie	The Hon Mrs F. Hopkinson
Gwibernant Ashley Robb	D	Mr W. C. Sloan	Mr P. A. Huet
Stanleyregis Premier	D	Mr P. Wilkins	Mr P. Wilkins
Ballyrobert Bess	B	Mr R. E. Clemitson	Mr R. E. Clemitson
Robbie of Barnacre	D	Mr H. Jackson	Mr H. Jackson
Philray Tern	D	Mrs E. M. Hartt	Mr P. R. Elsey
Criffel Ruth	B	Mr T. B. Laird	Mr T. B. Laird
Berrystead Factor	D	Mr W. C. Williams	Mr W. C. Williams
Coppicewood Carla	B	Capt. C. E. Owen	Mr T. Lawton Evans
Ballyrobert Chris	D	Mr R. E. Clemitson	Mr R. E. Clemitson
Lewstan Paul	D	Mr S. Lewis	Mr H. T. Hardwicke
Staxigoe Swing	D	Mr D. Mackenzie	Mr D. Mackenzie
Bricksclose Scout	D	Mrs M. Pratt	Mr J. S. Davis
Ballyrobert Clare	B	Mr R. E. Clemitson	Mr S. J. Burrows
Superscot Scamper	D	Mr. H. Watt	Mr W. Bremner
Criffel Cherry	B	Mr T. B. Laird	Mr T. B. Laird

Burnhatch Soda	D	Capt. S. Marriott	The Hon. F. Hopkinson
Crowhill Sal	B	Mr W. Anderson	Mr & Mrs J. S. Jenkins
Viewmount Vandal	D	Mr M. M. Jamieson	Mr M. M. Jamieson
Farway Skipper	D	Mr T. B. Healy	Mr T. B. Healy
Farway Shann	B	Mr T. B. Healy	Mr T. B. Healy
Crowhill Raffle	D	Mr A. Townson	Mr P. Stewart
Staxigoe Skimmer	B	Mr D. Mackenzie	Mr W. Bremner
Highland Boy	D	Mr J. Orr	Mr J. Orr
Meadowcourt Wendy	B	Mr R. Fairfax Naylor	Mr E. R. George
Ballyrobert Ben	D	Mr R. E. Clemitson	Mr J. Magee
Sprig of Inler	B	Mr J. Orr	Mr J. Orr
Harwes Silver	B	Mr R. McIntosh	Dr D. Bovill
Rytex Rex	D	Mr D. Pemberton	Mr R. Fairfax Naylor
Braiswood Rivet of Copford	D	Mrs E. M. Hartt	Mr R. King
Sport of Roffey	D	Mr C. Lawton Evans	Mr D. Cook
Pinewarren Cannonfire	D	Mr P. G. Wilkins	Dr N. O. Jones
Crowhill Spinner	B	Mr P. Stewart	Mr K. Erlandson
Braiswood Mattie	B	Mrs E. M. Hartt	Mrs E. M. Hartt
Smoke of Gorsty	B	Mrs D. B. Gaskell	Mrs D. B. Gaskell
Beeholme Heidi	B	Mr & Mrs A. Hurst	Mr R. T. Eagles
Bursilton Bramble	D	Mr I. Bowie	Mr I. Bowie
Scud of Pinewarren	D	Mr A. Chippett	Mr J. Cook
Barneys Blunder	D	Mr J. Crookshanks	Mr J. Crookshanks
Donna of Dewfield	B	Mrs E. M. Hartt	Mr J. F. Lock
Nell of Bellever	B	Mr A. B. Trevellion	Mr R. Hill
Trehayes Snowflake	B	Mr A. B. Trevellion	Mr A. B. Trevillion
Tripwire Twia	B	Mr & Mrs J. Carter	Mrs M. J. Carter
Concraig Bess	B	Mr W. Bremner	Mr C. Bremner
Ashley Buster	D	Mr A. B. Trevillion	Mr C. R. Burgoyne
Jay Mag	B	Mr D. Baird	Mr D. Baird
Don of Bronton	D	Mr T. B. Healy	Mr S. C. Lloyd
Burgiemains Dulnain of Staxigoe	B	Mrs Lahore	The Hon. Mrs F. Hopkinson
Santa Nick	D	Mrs Graham	Mrs C. Vale
Cleo of Coppicewood	B	Mrs E. M. Hartt	Mr C. Lawton Evans
Gorsty Greyling	D	Mrs D. Acheson	Mrs D. Acheson
Wigeon of Bellever	B	Mr T. B. Healy	Mr R. Hill
Judy of Runwell	B	Mr T. W. Pinner	Mr B. De'ath
Lyvennet Scamp	D	Mr & Mrs R. J. M. Dent	Mr & Mrs R. J. M. Dent
Kimble Kim	D	Mr P. Clulee	Mr R. A. Longville
Quarrybrae Mark	D	Mr W. Davidson	Mr B. Adamson

Appendix 4

Post-World War II Show Champions

Name	Sex	Breeder	Owner
Sandylands Show Girl	B	Mr M. D. Withers	Mrs G. Broadley
Starshine of Ide	D	Mr M. D. Withers	Mr J. H. J. Braddon
Sandylands Sherry	B	Mrs G. Broadley	Mrs G. Broadley
Carnfield Christabelle	B	Mr H. Jarvis	Mrs R. Perridge
Sandylands Shot	D	Mrs G. Broadley	Mrs G. Broadley
Skipper of Happeedaze	D	Mr W. R. Hepplewhite	Mr R. G. Thomas
Cavehill Maid	B	Mr W. R. Gardiner	Mr W. R. Gardiner
Grand Lodge	D	Miss E. Gault	Mr R. Cleland
Whintonhill Tessa	B	Mr W. R. Johnston	Messrs W. R. & J. Johnston
Roundwood Haynford Lady	B	Mr I. T. Whitaker	Mr & Mrs S. H. Till
Ambergris Alert	B	Miss D. Cupit	Miss D. Cupit
Banker of Bramhope	D	Miss E. McShane	Miss B. Cripps
Deana of Glenbervie	B	Miss A. Steele	Mr A. B. Nicholson
Sandylands Secret	B	Mrs G. Broadley	Mrs G. Broadley
My Love of Bourneview	B	Mr H. Hunt	Mr H. Hunt
Whaddon Chase Romance	B	Lady Lambe	Lady Lambe
Northdown Fancy	B	Mr W. E. Manin	Mr W. E. Manin
Wollburn Wallflower	B	Mrs H. M. S. Bell	Mrs H. M. S. Bell
Studley Brave Buccaneer	D	Mrs S. G. Smithson	Mrs S. G. Smithson
Hazel of Stubham	B	Mrs F. O. Till	Mrs F. O. Till
Bonaventure of Bramhope	D	Mrs E. A. T. Sawter	Mr E. E. A. Stevenson
Stokeley Sea Sprite	D	Mr D. C. Hannah	Mr D. C. Hannah
Pride of Abbotscross	B	Mr J. Orr	Mr T. Gordon
Mallard of Glenbervie	D	Mr A. B. Nicholson	Mr A. B. Nicholson
Jessica of Stubham	B	Mrs F. O. Till	Mr J. G. Lewis
Mably Sharon	B	Mr F. L. Martin	Mr J. Williams
Brandyhole Berry Brown	B	Mrs J. Spence	Mrs I. Durie
Onyx of Stubham	B	Mrs F. O. Till	Mr A. Wright
Whaddon Chase Salote	B	Lady Lambe	Lady Lambe
Brown Bess of Bramhope	B	Mrs S. G. Smithson	Mrs M. C. Scott
Beauvallet of Crosslane	D	Mr E. A. Anderson	Mr E. A. Anderson
Stokeley Sea Princess	B	Mr D. C. Hannah	Mr D. C. Hannah
Colmaris Nice Fella	D	Mr I. Davies	Mr I. Davies
Studley Debutante	B	Mrs S. G. Smithson	Mrs S. G. Smithson
Sheilah of Stubham	B	Mrs A. Redlich	Mrs F. O. Till
Colmaris Ranger	D	Mr I. Davies	Mr I. Davies
Vanity Fair of Stubham	B	Mrs F. O. Till	Mrs F. Sherwood
Glencora Country Maid	B	Mr J. Auld	Mr J. Auld
Judith of Cloudbrook	B	Mr K. Jones	Mr K. Jones
Glenford Gamester	D	Mr H. F. Lock	Mr H. F. Lock
Colmaris Bonny Lad	D	Mr I. Davies	Mr D. C. Hannah

Sandylands Susanna	B Mrs G. Broadley	Mrs G. Broadley & Miss A. Woolgar
Dovehouse Wonder Boy	D Mrs B. Lancashire	Miss J. Manifold
Stokeley Carmen	B Mr D.C. Hannah	Mr I. Davies
Moorcliff Keeper	D Mr E. Froggatt	Mr E. Froggatt
Studley Oscar	D Mrs S. G. Smithson	Mrs S. G. Smithson
Scarlet Ribbons of Stubham	B Mr A. Stevenson	Mrs F. O. Till
Wollburn Water Music	B Mrs H. M. S. Bell	Mrs H. M. S. Bell
Benefactor of Roundfield	D Mr J. G. Lewis	Mr J. G. Lewis
Pencloe Driftwood	D Miss M. H. Bolton	Miss M. H. Bolton
O'Malleys Tango of Glenbervie	B Mr W. J. McCall	Mr A. B. Nicholson
Pencloe Dynamo	D Miss M. H. Bolton	Miss M. H. Bolton
Conneil Covergirl	B Mrs C. Crawford	Mr & Mrs A. Bower
Lessudden Linnet	B Mrs R. Clark	Miss M. Alder
Woodbay Prima Donna	B Mrs F. Sherwood & Mr W. E. Manin	Mrs F. Sherwood
Douglas of Freetwood	D Mr J. Auld	Mr A. Stevenson
Weaversvale Luckystar	B Mr A. G. Nicholls	Mr A. G. Nicholls
Paidmyre Mallard	D Mr J. Lynch	Mr A. Stevenson
Rollencourt Danny Boy	D Mr F. Newsham	Mrs D. M. Senior
Elmerglade Early Dawn	B Mrs R. Campion	Mrs R. Campion
Whaddon Chase Drake	D Lady Lambe	Lady Lambe
Witching Eye of Freetwood	B Mr A. Stevenson	Mr J. Lindsay
Moorcliff Wigeon	B Mr E. Froggatt	Mr E. Froggatt
Kennersleigh Drummer Boy	D Mrs M. Keighley	Mrs M. Keighley
Moorcliff Freetwood Gamecock	D Mr A. Stevenson	Mr E. Froggatt
Lochardils Ghillie of Bramhope	D Mr A. Wylie	Mrs M. C. Scott
Dulcie of Kennersleigh	B Mrs M. Keighley	Mrs J. M. Taylor
Linzy Maid	B Mr A. Lindsay	Mr A. Lindsay
Moorcliff Bye Bye of Bramhope	B Mrs M. C. Scott	Mr E. Froggatt
Water Gypsy of Stubham	B Mrs F. O. Till	Mr & Mrs R. Townley
Slayleigh Paulina	B Major A. W. G. Scott	Mrs J. A. Hancock
Bella Bee of Kennersleigh	B Mrs M. Keighley	Mrs J. M. Taylor
Cavalier of Loweview	D Mr C. P. Jackson	Mr C. P. Jackson
Persimmon of Shipden	D Mr & Mrs C. J. Muirhead	Mr & Mrs C. J. Muirhead
Lisdalgin Babbling Brook	B Mr W. McClenaghan	Mr W. McClenaghan
Miss Chataway	B Miss M. H. Bolton	Miss M. H. Bolton
Majeba Mac	D Mr A. Wylie	Mr & Mrs J. Backhouse
Hawkhill Derby Daydream	B Mrs J. A. Hancock & Mr J. P. Cudworth	Miss F. Bagshawe
Cleavehill Dandini	D Mrs J. M. Taylor	Mrs J. M. Taylor
Moorcliff Camilla	B Mr E. Froggatt	Mr E. Froggatt
Sapphire of Shipden	B Mr & Mrs C. J. Muirhead	Mr A. C. Fowle
Hawkhill Royal Palace	D Mrs J. A. Hancock & Mr J. P. Cudworth	Mrs J. A. Hancock & Mr J. P. Cudworth
Hawkhill Hello Dolly	B Mrs Buchan	Mrs J. A. Hancock

Teesview Tarama	B Mrs E. Dobson	Mrs E. Dobson
Hawkhill St Pauli Girl of Moorcliff	B Mrs J. A. Hancock & Mr J. P. Cudworth	Mr E. Froggatt
Stokeley Son of Laddie	D Mr D. C. Hannah	Mrs K. Hannah
Whadhill Alicia	B Mrs E. Stephenson	Miss V. Phillips
Wollburn Wild Drake	D Mr C. Campbell	Mr R. L. Davies
Cleavehill Corn Dolly	B Mrs J. M. Taylor	Mrs J. M. Taylor
Lady Caroline of Hortonbank	B Mr L. Charlesworth	Mrs L. W. Carstairs
Woodbay Don Derry	D Mr V. Thomas	Mrs F. Sherwood
Hawkhill Connaught	D Mrs J. A. Hancock & Mr J. P. Cudworth	Mrs J. A. Hancock & Mr J. P. Cudworth
Elizabeth of Hortonbank	B Mr L. Charlesworth	Mrs J. Boyce
Hawkhill Harmonious	B Mrs J. A. Hancock	Mrs H. Jackson
Gewdore Apollo of Moorcliff	D Mr R. K. Robertson	Mrs J. Froggatt
Fairleigh Chocolate Bar	B Mrs J. Boyce	Mrs J. Boyce
Fairleigh Trentside	D Mrs J. Boyce	Mrs J. Boyce
Teesview Pandora of Truelindale	B Miss M. Alder	Mrs E. Dobson
Whitemoor Lady Diane	Mrs. W. Carstairs	Mrs L. W. Carstairs
Hawkhill Prince Consort of Moorcliff	D Mrs J. A. Hancock & Mr J. P. Cudworth	Mr E. Froggatt
Cleavehill Brigadier	D Mrs J. M. Taylor	Mrs E. W. Taylor
Mompesson Midsummer Dream	D Mrs F. Cottrell	Mrs F. Cotterell
Hawkhill Humble Duty	B Mrs J. A. Hancock	Mr & Mrs N. Hunton Morgans
Teesview Twister	D Mrs E. Dobson	Mr L. Soley
Cleavehill Tartan Arrow	D Mrs J. M. Taylor	Mrs J. M. Taylor
Cleavehill Islay Lass	B Mrs J. M. Taylor	Mrs J. M. Taylor
Woodbay Dianes Dilly	B Mrs F. Sherwood	Mrs F. Sherwood
Moorcliff Regent	D Mr & Mrs E. Froggatt	Mr R. W. Jackson
Majeba Meadow Mint	B Mr & Mrs J. Backhouse	Mr L. Antcliff
Hawkhill Finlandia	D Mrs J. A. Hancock	Mrs J. A. Hancock & Mr J. P. Cudworth
Chevalaux Crown Prince	D Mr & Mrs P. Dineen	Mr & Mrs P. Dineen
Hawkhill Happy Memory	B Mrs J. A. Hancock & Mr J. P. Cudworth	Mrs J. A. Hancock & Mr J. P. Cudworth
Barlochan Bellringer	B Mrs B. R. Lillie	Mrs B. R. Lillie
Corrigil Starshine	B Mr L. Soley	Mr P. Wood
Whitemoor Idle Chat	D Mrs L. W. Carstairs	Mrs L. W. Carstairs
Trand Bren Ragapple	B Mr J. Chadburn	Mr E. Chadburn
Irbyfield Commodore of Cleavehill	D Miss S. Martin	Mrs M. Lyons
Hildarry Roast Chesnut	B Mr H. Warmsley	Mrs D. A. Bury
Feorlig Beautiful Memory	B Mr & Mrs D. Miller	Mr & Mrs D. Miller
Michael of Blacon	D Mr & Mrs M. Roberts	Mr K. M. Morley
Moorcliff Sunnymaid	B Mr & Mrs E. Froggatt	Mr R. W. Jackson
St Trillos Grecian Girl	B Mrs K. M. Norman	Mrs K. M. Norman
Mastermind of Mordax	D Mr S. P. Cule	Mrs J. Cule
Grand Black Rod	D Mr R. Cleland	Mr R. Cleland
Amethyst of Lumb	B Mr D. Short	Mr E. Woodall
Rebecca of Knightward	B Mr J. G. Cooper	Mesdames Howard & McKnight

Sotherton Skywarrior	D Mr & Mrs B. Smith	Mr & Mrs B. Smith
Cleavehill Yankee Clipper	D Mrs J. M. Taylor	Mr E. W. Taylor
Whitemoor Idle Rich	D Mrs L. W. Carstairs	Mrs L. W. Carstairs
Cholesbury Seabird	B Mr W. Arnott	Mrs V. G. Burhouse
Mompesson Wonderful Dream	B Mrs F. Cottrell	Mrs F. Cottrell
Mompesson Sleeping Partner	B Mrs J. A. Hancock & Mr J. P. Cudworth	Mrs F. Cottrell
Cleavehill Tartan Special	D Mrs J. M. Taylor	Mrs J. M. Taylor
Star of the Moss	D Mr J. Sharpe	Messrs T. & W. McBlain
Feorlig Firenza of Pencloe	D Mr & Mrs D. Miller	Miss M. H. Bolton
Hawkhill Riding Low	B Mrs E. Dobson & Mr D. L'Anson	Mrs E. Dobson & Mr D. L'Anson
Monclare Mr Chips	D Mr & Mrs I. Sharples	Mr & Mrs I. Sharples & Mr C. P. Jackson
Cleavehill Harvest Gold	D Mrs J. M. Taylor	Mrs J. M. Taylor
Verulam Liver Pate	B Mr K. R. Payne	Mr & Mrs K. R. Payne

Appendix 5

Bibliography of Field Training Books

Carlton, H. W., *Spaniels: Their Breaking for Sport and Field Trials* (Harmsworth Press)
Erlandson, Keith, *Gundog Training* (Barrie and Jenkins)
Hopper, Maurice, *Spaniel Training for Modern Shooters* (David and Charles)
Moxon, P. R. A., *Gundogs: Training and Field Trials* (Popular Dogs)
Radcliffe, Talbot, *Spaniels for Sport* (Faber and Faber)

Index